New Longman Shakespeare

A Midsummer Night's Dream

William Shakespeare

edited by John O'Connor

D0177247

Longman

Edinburgh Gate
Harlow, Essex

Pearson Education Limited
Edinburgh Gate
Harlow
Essex
CM20 2JE
England and Associated Companies throughout the World

© Pearson Education Limited 2000

All rights reserved. No part of this publication may be
reproduced, stored in a retrieval system, or transmitted
in any form or by any means, electronic, mechanical,
photocopying, recording, or otherwise without the prior
permission of the Publishers or a licence permitting
restricted copying in the United Kingdom issued by the
Copyright Leasing Agency Ltd, 90 Tottenham Court Road,
London, W1P 0LP.

ISBN: 0582–42712–6

First published 2000
Fourth impression 2003
Printed in Singapore (MPM)

The Publisher's policy is to use paper manufactured from
sustainable forests.

Acknowledgements
We are grateful to the following for permission to reproduce
photographs and artwork:

Anthony Crickmay/The Shakespeare Birthplace Trust 28;
Clive Barda/The Shakespeare Birthplace Trust 20, 26, 48, 68,
84; Donald Cooper/The Shakespeare Birthplace Trust 34, 90;
Geraint Lewis/The Shakespeare Birthplace Trust 26, 82, 114,
144; Ivan Kyncl/The Shakespeare Birthplace Trust 134; The
Shakespeare Birthplace Trust/Joe Cocks 60, 104; The
Shakespeare Birthplace Trust/Malcolm Davies 112, 122, 140;
NVC Arts/Glyndebourne Productions Ltd 154

Cover: Robbie Jack Photography

Contents

Introduction   iv

Characters in the play   1

Notes and activities   2
A Midsummer Night's Dream   3

Activities: Thinking about the play as a whole   152
     Actors' interpretations   152
     Character reviews   154
     Shakespeare's language   159
     Themes   159
     Plot review   160

Background to Shakespeare and *A Midsummer Night's Dream*   161
     Shakespeare's England   161
     Plays and playhouses   163
     The Globe theatre   166
     The social background   169
     Shakespeare's verse   171
     The plot of *A Midummer Night's Dream*   174
     Study skills: titles and quotations   178
     William Shakespeare and *A Midsummer Night's Dream*   179

Index of activities   182

Introduction

To the student

Shakespeare wrote *A Midsummer Night's Dream* so that it could be performed by actors and enjoyed by audiences. To help you get the most out of the play, this edition includes:
- a complete **script**
- **notes** printed next to the script which explain difficulties and point out important features
- **activities** on the same page which will help you to focus on the scene you are reading
- page-by-page **summaries** on the plot
- **exam questions** after each Act, which will give you practice at the right level
- **background information** about *A Midsummer Night's Dream*, Shakespeare's theatre and the verse he uses
- **advice** on how to set out titles and quotations in your essays.

To the teacher

New Longman Shakespeare has been designed to meet the varied and complex needs of students working throughout the 11–16 age range.

The textual notes

These have been newly written to provide understandable explanations which are easily located on the page:
- notes are placed next to the text with clear line references
- explanations of more complex words are given in context and help is provided with key imagery and historical reference

The activities

1 **Activities accompanying the text**
These are based on the premise that the text is best enjoyed and understood as a script for performance:

- In addition to a wide variety of reading, writing, listening and speaking activities, students are encouraged to: improvise, learn the script for performance, freeze-frame, rehearse, hot-seat, devise graphs and charts and create various forms of artwork, including storyboards, collages and cartoons.
- To provide a clear structure, activities are placed opposite the section of text to which they refer and come under five headings:

  i **Character reviews** help students to think about the many different aspects of a given character which are presented in the course of the play. There might be as many as twenty of these activities on a single major character.

  ii **Actors' interpretations** draw upon actual performances and ask students to consider comments from actors and directors in film and stage productions.

  iii **Shakespeare's language** activities, focusing on everything from imagery to word-play, enable students to understand how the dramatist's language works to convey the central ideas of the play.

  iv **Plot reviews** help students to keep in mind the essential details of what is happening in the story as well as asking them to consider how the plot is structured.

  v **Themes** are explored according to their predominance in each play.

- 'Serial activities' (Hermia 1, ... 2, ... 3, for example) enable students to focus in detail on a single key feature.

In addition, students who find extended tasks on Shakespeare a daunting prospect can combine several of these more focused activities – each in itself free-standing – to form the basis of a fuller piece of work.

2 **Exam-style activities**

At the end of each act – and also at the end of the book – there are activities which require SATs and GCSE style responses and offer opportunities for assessment.

3 **Summative activities**

Thinking about the play as a whole... is a section which offers a wide range of summative activities suitable for all levels.

Differentiation

Many students using this edition will be approaching Shakespeare for the first time; some might be studying the play for their Key Stage 3 SATs exam; others will be working towards GCSE.

To answer their very different needs and interests, many of the activities have been differentiated to match the National Curriculum Level Descriptions and GCSE criteria. Activities of this kind are presented in three levels:

A Foundation level activities, which support an initial reading of the play and help students to build a solid basic knowledge and understanding

B Activities geared towards the needs of Year 9 Key Stage 3 students preparing for SATs

C More advanced activities in line with GCSE requirements.

Plot summaries

As students work through the play, their understanding of the play's plot is supported by:
- a brief headline summary at the top of each spread
- regular Plot Review activities
- a final detailed summary, scene by scene.

Background

Detailed fact-sheets are provided on:
- Shakespeare's England
- Plays and playhouses
- The Globe theatre
- The social and historical background (to each particular play)
- Shakespeare's life and his times.

Studying and writing about the play

To help students who are studying the play for examinations, there are sections on:
- Shakespeare's verse (with examples from the particular play)
- Study skills: titles and quotations.

Characters in the play

The Athenian court
THESEUS *Duke of Athens*
HIPPOLYTA *Queen of the Amazons, engaged to Theseus*
EGEUS *a lord, Hermia's father*
PHILOSTRATE *the Master of the Revels*

The lovers
HERMIA *Egeus's daughter*
HELENA
LYSANDER
DEMETRIUS *Egeus's choice of husband for Hermia*

The mechanicals (Athenian workmen)	*their parts in* *'Pyramus and Thisby'*
PETER QUINCE *a carpenter*	the Prologue
NICK BOTTOM *a weaver*	Pyramus
FRANCIS FLUTE *a bellows-mender*	Thisby
TOM SNOUT *a tinker*	Wall
ROBIN STARVELING *a tailor*	Moonshine
SNUG *a joiner*	Lion

The fairies
PUCK *also called Robin Goodfellow*
OBERON *King of the fairies*
TITANIA *Queen of the fairies*
PEASEBLOSSOM }
COBWEB   } *Titania's*
MOTH   } *attendants*
MUSTARDSEED }
A FAIRY *in Titania's service*

Other lords and ladies from the Athenian court

The story takes place in Athens and a nearby wood.

1.1 Theseus's palace in Athens

Theseus, Duke of Athens, is talking to Hippolyta, Queen of the Amazons, about their marriage, when they are interrupted by Egeus, his daughter Hermia and two young men. Egeus wants Hermia to marry Demetrius, but complains that Lysander has won her affections by bewitching her.

Activities

Themes: love (1)

Courtship and marriage
In pairs, re-read lines 1–19 and discuss any difficult words and phrases. Then act out the exchange between Theseus and Hippolyta, bringing out his impatience and her patience.

Shakespeare's language: the moon

The moon has always had a special significance for people in all cultures and is referred to many times in this play.

1. How many nursery rhymes or popular songs can you think of which feature the moon?
2. What significance do you attach to:
   - the moon and 'madness' (where does the word 'lunatic' come from?)?
   - the moon's influence on the earth (think about tides)?
   - the moon and the calendar?
   - the moon and chastity (it will help to read the section about the goddess Diana on page 170)?

As you read the play, look out for the references to the moon and its connections with (a) odd behaviour; and (b) chastity.

1–2 **our nuptial … apace** it will soon be our wedding day

2–3 **Four happy … moon** it will be a new moon in four days' time

4 **wanes** decreases in size
lingers my desires delays me in what I want to do

5 **step-dame … dowager** step-mother … widow

6 **Long withering out … revenue** *If a young man's father remarried, or if his widowed mother lived a long time, all the fortune that he hoped to inherit might be used up.*

7 **steep** bathe; *the days will fade into night*

11 **solemnities** marriage ceremony

13 **pert** brisk and lively

14 **Turn melancholy forth** reject gloominess

15 **The pale companion … pomp** There is no place for melancholy in our ceremonies

16–17 **I wooed thee … injuries** *Theseus had defeated Hippolyta, Queen of the Amazons, in battle.*

19 **triumph** public shows of rejoicing

20 **renowned** famous

22 **vexation** irritation, annoyance

27 **bewitched the bosom** won her heart by magic charms

28 **rhymes** love poems

29 **interchanged** exchanged

Act 1

Scene 1

Athens.

Enter THESEUS, HIPPOLYTA, PHILOSTRATE, *and* ATTENDANTS.

THESEUS   Now, fair Hippolyta, our nuptial hour
Draws on apace: four happy days bring in
Another moon: but O, methinks how slow
This old moon wanes; she lingers my desires
Like to a step-dame, or a dowager,   5
Long withering out a young man's revenue.

HIPPOLYTA   Four days will quickly steep themselves in night;
Four nights will quickly dream away the time;
And then the moon, like to a silver bow
New bent in heaven, shall behold the night   10
Of our solemnities.

THESEUS   Go, Philostrate,
Stir up the Athenian youth to merriments;
Awake the pert and nimble spirit of mirth;
Turn melancholy forth to funerals:
The pale companion is not for our pomp.   15

Exit PHILOSTRATE.

Hippolyta, I wooed thee with my sword,
And won thy love doing thee injuries;
But I will wed thee in another key,
With pomp, with triumph, and with revelling.

Enter EGEUS *and his daughter* HERMIA, LYSANDER, *and* DEMETRIUS.

EGEUS   Happy be Theseus, our renownéd Duke!   20

THESEUS   Thanks, good Egeus: what's the news with thee?

EGEUS   Full of vexation come I, with complaint
Against my child, my daughter Hermia.
Stand forth, Demetrius. My noble lord,
This man hath my consent to marry her.   25
Stand forth, Lysander; and, my gracious Duke,
This man hath bewitched the bosom of my child:
Thou, thou Lysander, thou hast given her rhymes,
And interchanged love-tokens with my child:

1.1 Theseus's palace in Athens

Egeus wants to enforce an old law: either his daughter marries Demetrius or is condemned to death. When Theseus reminds Hermia of her duty to her father, she tells Theseus of her love for Lysander.

Activities

Character review: Hermia (1)

'I know not by what power I am made bold ...'
Hermia's father is not permitting her to marry Lysander because he wants her to marry Demetrius. To understand the difficult position that Hermia is in, re-read Theseus's words about fathers (lines 47–51) and the section about fathers and daughters on page 169.

1. How do you think Theseus expects her to behave?
2. What is surprising about (a) Hermia's refusal to marry Demetrius and (b) the way in which Hermia replies to Theseus here?

Themes: love (2)

'Thou hast given her rhymes ...'
After Egeus's comic account of Lysander's wooing, his threats to Hermia concerning the Athenian law can be quite shocking. Perform Egeus's speech so as to bring out the comedy of lines 28–38 (the exaggerated descriptions) and the full seriousness of lines 38–45 (his threats).

31 **feigning ... feigning** (1) soft (*in voice*); (2) deceitful (*pretending to lover her*)

32 **stolen ... fantasy** won over her impressionable heart

33–34 *Lysander is accused of having given Hermia rings, flashy gifts* (**gauds**), *trinkets* (**conceits**), *knick-knacks, little presents* (**trifles**), *flowers* (**nosegays**) *and sweets.*

34–35 **messengers ... youth** things which are likely to have a strong influence on a young, innocent girl

36 **filched** stolen

38 **harshness** disobedience

39 **Be it so** if, supposing

41 **privilege** right

45 **Immediately ... case** expressly provided for in cases like this

46 **Be advised** think carefully

49 **form** pattern, design

51 **figure** picture

54 **in this kind ... voice** in his present position, not having your father's support

56 **would** wish

58 **entreat** beg

60 **concern** suit

63 **befall** happen to

65 **abjure** give up (*by becoming a nun*)

Thou hast by moonlight at her window sung, 30
With feigning voice, verses of feigning love,
And stolen the impression of her fantasy
With bracelets of thy hair, rings, gawds, conceits,
Knacks, trifles, nosegays, sweetmeats, messengers
Of strong prevailment in unhardened youth; 35
With cunning hast thou filched my daughter's heart,
Turned her obedience, which is due to me,
To stubborn harshness. And, my gracious Duke,
Be it so she will not here before your Grace
Consent to marry with Demetrius, 40
I beg the ancient privilege of Athens;
As she is mine, I may dispose of her;
Which shall be either to this gentleman,
Or to her death, according to our law
Immediately provided in that case. 45

THESEUS   What say you, Hermia? Be advised, fair maid.
To you your father should be as a god;
One that composed your beauties; yea, and one
To whom you are but as a form in wax
By him imprinted; and within his power 50
To leave the figure, or disfigure it.
Demetrius is a worthy gentleman.

HERMIA   So is Lysander.

THESEUS   In himself he is;
But in this kind, wanting your father's voice,
The other must be held the worthier. 55

HERMIA   I would my father looked but with my eyes.

THESEUS   Rather your eyes must with his judgement look.

HERMIA   I do entreat your Grace to pardon me.
I know not by what power I am made bold,
Nor how it may concern my modesty 60
In such a presence here to plead my thoughts;
But I beseech your Grace, that I may know
The worst that may befall me in this case,
If I refuse to wed Demetrius.

THESEUS   Either to die the death, or to abjure 65

1.1 Theseus's palace in Athens

Theseus confirms that Hermia has three choices: to marry Demetrius, become a nun, or suffer the death penalty. The two young men each argue why they should be allowed to marry her.

Activities

Character review: Theseus (1)

'What say you, Hermia? Be advised, fair maid ...'

What is Theseus's view of the position that Hermia is in? Is he on Egeus's side? Does he approve of the harsh Athenian law? In pairs, act out Theseus's words to Hermia in a number of different ways, for example, as though he is:

- in agreement with Egeus, and threatening Hermia
- in agreement with Egeus, but trying to persuade Hermia with commonsense points
- not in agreement with Egeus, but diplomatically trying to hide the fact that he supports Hermia
- openly showing that he is not in agreement with Egeus.

Theseus says: (line 72) as a nun, Hermia would not be allowed to marry and have children; (line 74) people who control their passions in that way are trebly blessed; (line 76) but a woman's beauty can be handed on to her children, just as a rose's scent can be distilled to make perfume; (lines 88–90) so Hermia must marry Demetrius or swear on the altar of the goddess of chastity to live a strict, unmarried life for ever.

67–68 **question ... blood** think about what you really want, consider how young you are, examine your feelings

69 **yield not** do not give in to

70 **endure the livery** tolerate the dress

71 **For aye... mewed** to be shut up forever in a dark nunnery

73 **fruitless** barren *(see line 72); the moon was associated with Diana, goddess of chastity*

75 **maiden pilgrimage** the holy travels (= *life*) of a virgin

76 **earthlier happy** happier on earth

80 **Ere** before

virgin patent my right to keep my virginity

81–82 **Unto his ... sovereignty** *As Hermia's soul has refused to accept Demetrius as its lord, she will not give up her virginity to him either.*

83 **pause** think things over

84 **sealing-day** day when we sign the (marriage) contract

88 **would** wishes

92 **crazéd title** unsound claim

94 **do you ...** *(not a question:)* You marry him!

96 **render** give

98 **estate unto** give formally to

99 **as well derived** from as good a family

100 **as well possessed** as wealthy

102 **with vantage** better

For ever the society of men.
Therefore, fair Hermia, question your desires,
Know of your youth, examine well your blood.
Whether, if you yield not your father's choice,
You can endure the livery of a nun, 70
For aye to be in shady cloister mewed,
To live a barren sister all your life,
Chanting faint hymns to the cold fruitless moon.
Thrice blessèd they that master so their blood
To undergo such maiden pilgrimage; 75
But earthlier happy is the rose distilled
Than that which, withering on the virgin thorn,
Grows, lives, and dies in single blessedness.

HERMIA   So will I grow, so live, so die, my lord,
Ere I will yield my virgin patent up 80
Unto his lordship, whose unwishèd yoke,
My soul consents not to give sovereignty.

THESEUS   Take time to pause, and by the next new moon,
The sealing-day betwixt my love and me
For everlasting bond of fellowship, 85
Upon that day either prepare to die
For disobedience to your father's will,
Or else to wed Demetrius as he would,
Or on Diana's altar to protest
For aye austerity and single life. 90

DEMETRIUS   Relent, sweet Hermia, and Lysander, yield
Thy crazèd title to my certain right.

LYSANDER   You have her father's love, Demetrius:
Let me have Hermia's; do you marry him.

EGEUS   Scornful Lysander, true, he hath my love; 95
And what is mine my love shall render him;
And she is mine, and all my right of her
I do estate unto Demetrius.

LYSANDER   I am, my Lord, as well derived as he,
As well possessed; my love is more than his; 100
My fortunes every way as fairly ranked,
If not with vantage, as Demetrius';
And, which is more than all these boasts can be,

1.1 Theseus's palace in Athens

Lysander points out that Demetrius has been wooing a young woman called Helena, who loves him in return. When Theseus leaves, to discuss the situation with Egeus and Demetrius, Hermia and Lysander are left alone to bemoan their situation.

Activities

Actors' interpretations: 'What cheer, my love?'

1. What prompts Theseus to ask this question (line 122)? Is it something Hippolyta has done, or something about the way she is silently reacting? Has something upset her? In pairs, work out what you think this is all about and act out lines 111–126.

2. Improvise the conversation that Theseus has with Egeus and Demetrius after they leave. Are there any clues in lines 106–116 and 123–126?

Plot review (1): news from court

A In pairs, recap on the first few pages making sure that you can answer the following questions:

- How did Theseus meet Hippolyta and how did he woo her?
- Why is Egeus angry?
- How do Lysander and Demetrius fit into the picture?
- What connection does Helena (line 107) have with all this?

continued on page 10

105 **prosecute** take further

106 **avouch ... head** say it to his face

109 **in idolatry** *She worships Demetrius as a god.*

110 **spotted and inconstant** sinful and changeable

113 **self-affairs** my own personal matters

116 **private schooling** instructions to give you in private

117 **look you arm ...** make sure you are prepared

118 **your fancies** what you want to do

120 **Which ... extenuate** and I am powerless to relax the law

125 **Against our nuptial** in preparation for our wedding

126 **nearly that concerns** which closely concerns

130 **Belike** perhaps

131 **Beteem** (1) allow; (2) teem (pour down)

132 **for aught ... read** from anything I have ever read

135 **blood** birth (*social class and rank*)

136 **O cross! ... low** O what an obstacle! Being too high born to be enslaved by someone of lower rank!

137 **misgrafféd** badly matched

I am beloved of beauteous Hermia.
Why should not I then prosecute my right?   105
Demetrius, I'll avouch it to his head,
Made love to Nedar's daughter, Helena,
And won her soul: and she, sweet lady, dotes,
Devoutly dotes, dotes in idolatry,
Upon this spotted and inconstant man.   110

THESEUS   I must confess that I have heard so much,
And with Demetrius thought to have spoke thereof:
But being over-full of self-affairs,
My mind did lose it. But Demetrius, come,
And come Egeus, you shall go with me;   115
I have some private schooling for you both.
For you, fair Hermia, look you arm yourself
To fit your fancies to your father's will;
Or else the law of Athens yields you up –
Which by no means we may extenuate –   120
To death, or to a vow of single life.
Come, my Hippolyta; what cheer, my love?
Demetrius and Egeus, go along:
I must employ you in some business
Against our nuptial, and confer with you   125
Of something nearly that concerns yourselves.

EGEUS   With duty and desire we follow you.

Exeunt. LYSANDER *and* HERMIA *remain.*

LYSANDER   How now, my love? why is your cheek so pale?
How chance the roses there do fade so fast?

HERMIA   Belike for want of rain, which I could well   130
Beteem them from the tempest of my eyes.

LYSANDER   Ay me; for aught that I could ever read,
Could ever hear by tale or history,
The course of true love never did run smooth;
But either it was different in blood –   135

HERMIA   O cross! too high to be enthralled to low.

LYSANDER   Or else misgraffed, in respect of years. –

HERMIA   O spite! too old to be engaged to young.

1.1 Theseus's palace in Athens

Lysander has an idea, and suggests that he and Hermia should elope and stay with Lysander's aunt. She lives some way from Athens, and they can get married without breaking the law.

Activities

B 1. Write an article for the *Athens Independent* which covers the latest news from the court of Duke Theseus. (Many newspapers used to have a section called 'Court Circular', which provided news of the royal family.) Your article should cover:
   - the background to Theseus's courtship of Hippolyta (lines 16–17)
   - the preparations for the wedding (lines 11–15; 18–19)
   - the potential scandal concerning Hermia's refusal to marry Demetrius (lines 20–127).

2. Write Lysander's letter to his aunt, in which he explains all the circumstances and asks for her help.

C Write an entry in Hippolyta's private diary in which she:
   - gives her opinions on the dispute in court concerning Hermia
   - expresses her feelings about her coming marriage to Theseus.

How have Theseus's responses to Hermia's plight and his comments on the Athenian law affected Hippolyta's view of him?

143 **momentary** lasting only a moment

145 **collied** darkened, blackened

146 **spleen** fit of bad temper

149 **quick** (1) quickly; (2) alive

151 **edict in destiny** law of fate

153 **customary cross** the usual obstacle that lovers have to face

154 **due** fitting

155 **fancy's** love's

156 **persuasion** argument

157–158 **dowager Of great revenue** a wealthy widow

159 **leagues** *a league was roughly three miles*

165 **without** outside

167 **To do observance ...** to celebrate May-day

169 **Cupid's** *Cupid was the son of Venus, goddess of love (see line 171); he was usually portrayed as blindfolded, with a bow and arrow (see page 170).*

171 **doves** *Doves drew Venus's chariot.*

173–174 **the Carthage Queen ...** *Dido, Queen of Carthage, fell in love with Æneas (*the false Troyan*); when he deserted her, she threw herself on a funeral pyre (see page 170).*

LYSANDER	Or else it stood upon the choice of friends –
HERMIA	O hell! to choose love by another's eyes. 140

LYSANDER   Or, if there were a sympathy in choice,
War, death, or sickness did lay siege to it;
Making it momentary as a sound,
Swift as a shadow, short as any dream,
Brief as the lightning in the collied night,   145
That in a spleen unfolds both heaven and earth,
And ere a man hath power to say, Behold!
The jaws of darkness do devour it up;
So quick bright things come to confusion.

HERMIA   If then true lovers have been ever crossed,   150
It stands as an edict in destiny.
Then let us teach our trial patience,
Because it is a customary cross,
As due to love as thoughts, and dreams, and sighs,
Wishes and tears, poor fancy's followers.   155

LYSANDER   A good persuasion; therefore hear me, Hermia:
I have a widow aunt, a dowager
Of great revenue, and she hath no child;
From Athens is her house remote seven leagues,
And she respects me as her only son.   160
There, gentle Hermia, may I marry thee;
And to that place the sharp Athenian law
Cannot pursue us. If thou lov'st me, then,
Steal forth thy father's house tomorrow night;
And in the wood, a league without the town,   165
Where I did meet thee once with Helena
To do observance to a morn of May,
There will I stay for thee.

HERMIA   My good Lysander,
I swear to thee by Cupid's strongest bow,
By his best arrow with the golden head,   170
By the simplicity of Venus' doves,
By that which knitteth souls and prospers loves,
And by that fire which burned the Carthage Queen
When the false Troyan under sail was seen,
By all the vows that ever men have broke,   175
In number more than ever women spoke,

1.1 Theseus's palace in Athens

Hermia is excited by Lysander's plan and agrees to meet him the next night in the wood outside the city, from where they will make their escape. Helena arrives, miserable that Demetrius does not return her affections or find her beautiful, but loves Hermia instead.

Activities

Character review: Helena (1)

'Call you me fair?'

1. Re-read lines 180–201. Is Helena angry, bitter, jealous, bewildered …? To help you decide, perform the speech in different ways.
2. What are Helena's problems? Write a letter from Helena to a problem page in which she talks about her love for Demetrius and compares her own physical appearance with Hermia's.

Shakespeare's language: one-line speeches

Hermia's attempts to explain her relationship with Demetrius are met by quick, punchy replies from Helena (lines 184–201).

1. In pairs, re-read the exchange and jot down the points that the characters are making in each speech. Then improvise it in your own words.
2. Write a similar piece of dialogue in which Lysander tries to convince Egeus to let him marry Hermia. Use your own language or – if you are feeling confident – write in Shakespeare's verse (in which case it will help to read the section on pages 171–174 first).

180 **wither away?** where are you going?

181 **unsay** take it back, deny what you have said

fair Helena is (1) fair-skinned and blonde; (2) beautiful

182 **fair** beauty

183 **lode-stars** guiding stars

183 **air** tune

184 **tuneable** melodic, pleasant-sounding

186 **favour** physical appearance

190 **bated** excepted; *Hermia would give the whole world (except Demetrius) to be transformed (***translated***) into Hermia.*

192 **art** skill

201 **would** I wish

In that same place thou hast appointed me,
Tomorrow truly will I meet with thee.

LYSANDER   Keep promise, love. Look, here comes Helena.

Enter HELENA.

HERMIA   God speed, fair Helena, whither away?   180

HELENA   Call you me fair? That fair again unsay.
Demetrius loves your fair. O happy fair!
Your eyes are lode-stars, and your tongue's sweet air
More tuneable than lark to shepherd's ear,
When wheat is green, when hawthorn buds
    appear.   185
Sickness is catching; O, were favour so,
Yours would I catch, fair Hermia, ere I go.
My ear should catch your voice, my eye your eye,
My tongue should catch your tongue's sweet melody.
Were the world mine, Demetrius being bated,   190
The rest I'd give to be to you translated.
O teach me how you look and with what art
You sway the motion of Demetrius' heart!

HERMIA   I frown upon him, yet he loves me still.

HELENA   O that your frowns would teach my smiles such
    skill!   195

HERMIA   I give him curses, yet he gives me love.

HELENA   O that my prayers could such affection move!

HERMIA   The more I hate, the more he follows me.

HELENA   The more I love, the more he hateth me.

HERMIA   His folly, Helena, is no fault of mine.   200

HELENA   None but your beauty; would that fault were mine!

HERMIA   Take comfort: he no more shall see my face;
Lysander and myself will fly this place.
Before the time I did Lysander see,
Seemed Athens as a paradise to me.   205

1.1 Theseus's palace in Athens

Hermia and Lysander comfort Helena by revealing their plan to elope: they say this will leave the field free for her to win back Demetrius's affections. When they leave, Helena recalls how Demetrius used to think her beautiful.

Activities

Themes: love (3)

'Love can ...'

Helena's soliloquy includes her views on the experience of being in love and the effect it has on people's judgement (lines 232–245). Jot down her main points, paying particular attention to the following:

- What can love do to 'things base and vile' (lines 232–233)?
- Why is Cupid always shown blindfolded (lines 234–235)?
- What else does the picture of Cupid suggest about love (lines 236–241)?

Write a short poem, based upon the points she makes, in which each line starts with 'Love can ...' and states one of the things that love, according to Helena, is capable of doing. (It will help to read the notes about Cupid on pages 10 and 170.)

206 **graces** (1) attractive qualities; (2) the goodness of God

209–211 **when Phoebe ... grass** when the moon is reflected in the water and the dew is on the grass (*see page 170*)

212 **still** always

213 **devised to steal** planned to escape

215 **wont** accustomed, used

216 **emptying ... sweet** sharing sweet secrets

219 **stranger companies** the company of strangers

223 **lovers' food** the pleasure of seeing each other

225 **As you ...** May Demetrius dote as much on you as you do on him

226 **other some** some other people

230 **errs** does the wrong thing

235 **therefore is** that's why

236 **Nor hath ... taste** and love does not have a smattering of common sense

237 **figure** represent (*Cupid has wings and is blindfolded*)

239 **beguiled** cheated

240 **As waggish ...** just as playful boys break their promises ...

241 **is perjured** breaks his word

242 **ere** before

eyne eyes

O then, what graces in my love do dwell,
That he hath turned a heaven unto a hell!

LYSANDER   Helen, to you our minds we will unfold.
Tomorrow night, when Phoebe doth behold
Her silver visage in the watery glass,   210
Decking with liquid pearl the bladed grass,
A time that lovers' flights doth still conceal,
Through Athens' gates have we devised to steal.

HERMIA   And in the wood, where often you and I
Upon faint primrose-beds were wont to lie,   215
Emptying our bosoms of their counsel sweet,
There, my Lysander and myself shall meet,
And thence from Athens turn away our eyes
To seek new friends and stranger companies.
Farewell, sweet playfellow; pray thou for us;   220
And good luck grant thee thy Demetrius.
Keep word, Lysander; we must starve our sight
From lovers' food, till morrow deep midnight.

LYSANDER   I will, my Hermia. (*Exit* HERMIA) Helena, adieu.
As you on him, Demetrius dote on you!   225

                                              Exit LYSANDER.

HELENA   How happy some o'er other some can be!
Through Athens I am thought as fair as she.
But what of that? Demetrius thinks not so;
He will not know what all but he do know:
And as he errs, doting on Hermia's eyes,   230
So I, admiring of his qualities.
Things base and vile, holding no quantity,
Love can transpose to form and dignity.
Love looks not with the eyes, but with the mind,
And therefore is winged Cupid painted blind.   235
Nor hath Love's mind of any judgement taste;
Wings, and no eyes, figure unheedy haste;
And therefore is Love said to be a child,
Because in choice he is so oft beguiled.
As waggish boys in game themselves forswear;   240
So the boy Love is perjured everwhere;
For ere Demetrius looked on Hermia's eyne,
He hailed down oaths that he was only mine;

1.2 Peter Quince's house

Helena decides that, to earn Demetrius's gratitude, she will tell him about the planned elopement. Elsewhere in Athens, a group of workmen (the 'mechanicals') have met to rehearse a play, which they hope to perform on Theseus's wedding-night.

Activities

Shakespeare's language: names

Look at the opening stage directions to 1.2. Shakespeare has chosen names which have something to do with each character's trade:

- Bottom: a 'bottom' was the core on which the weaver's skein of yarn was wound
- Quince: 'quoins' are wooden wedges used by carpenters
- Snug: good joiners make snuggly-fitting joints
- Flute: a term connected with church organ pipes (which a bellows-mender would work on)
- Snout means nozzle or spout (something a tinker would mend)
- Starveling refers to the fact that tailors were famous for being skinny and feeble.

Make up some names which Shakespeare might have chosen for a group of workmen today, such as a plumber, an electrician, a gardener, a car mechanic or a builder. Don't make them too obvious and try to include some light-hearted reference to the trade in the name you choose.

245 **dissolved** (1) broke his promises; (2) melted with love

248 **intelligence** information

249 **dear expense** a trouble worth taking

250 **enrich my pain** get something out of the effort I'm making

2 **generally** *He means 'severally' (one at a time).*

3 **scrip** script

6 **interlude** short play

10 **point** conclusion

11 **Marry** (*a mild oath*) By Saint Mary!

   lamentable sad, mournful

12 **Pyramus and Thisbe** *well known lovers, from a popular ballad*

And when this hail some heat from Hermia felt,
So he dissolved, and showers of oaths did melt.   245
I will go tell him of fair Hermia's flight;
Then to the wood will he tomorrow night
Pursue her; and for this intelligence,
If I have thanks, it is a dear expense.
But herein mean I to enrich my pain,   250
To have his sight thither, and back again.

Exit.

Scene 2

Athens.

Enter QUINCE *the carpenter,* SNUG *the joiner,* BOTTOM *the weaver,*
FLUTE *the bellows-mender,* SNOUT *the tinker, and* STARVELING *the
tailor.*

QUINCE   Is all our company here?

BOTTOM   You were best to call them generally, man by man,
according to the scrip.

QUINCE   Here is the scroll of every man's name, which is
thought fit, through all Athens, to play in our   5
interlude before the Duke and the Duchess on his
wedding-day at night.

BOTTOM   First, good Peter Quince, say what the play treats on:
then read the names of the actors: and so grow to a
point.   10

QUINCE   Marry, our play is: 'The most lamentable comedy
and most cruel death of Pyramus and Thisby'.

BOTTOM   A very good piece of work, I assure you, and a
merry. Now, good Peter Quince, call forth your
actors by the scroll. Masters, spread yourselves.   15

QUINCE   Answer as I call you. Nick Bottom, the weaver.

BOTTOM   Ready; name what part I am for, and proceed.

QUINCE   You, Nick Bottom, are set down for Pyramus.

1.2 Peter Quince's house

The play is about two lovers, Pyramus and Thisby. Nick Bottom boasts how passionately he will play the part of Pyramus, but then decides that he wants to play Thisby too.

Activities

Character review: the mechanicals (1)

What are they like?

1. Later in the play, Puck calls this group 'rude mechanicals' (rough workmen), and this is the name by which audiences usually know them. What are the contrasts between the mechanicals and the court? Think about: their social class; their names (see the activity on page 16); their main interests; their problems and worries; the ways they speak.

2. Flute and Starveling play women's parts in the mechanicals' play, because women were not permitted to act on public stages in Shakespeare's time. In groups of four (ideally of mixed gender) talk about the preparations that Flute would need to make, to play a woman successfully. Think about (a) physical concerns (adapting his figure, voice, gestures, movements); and (b) psychological concerns ('thinking himself into' playing a woman). Since the 1660s, women have played the female characters, who often have to disguise themselves as males. Now think about the preparations women have to make to play men.

19 **lover … tyrant** *two popular stage characters*

23 **condole** express grief

24 **chief humour** main inclination; what I really feel suited for

25 **Ercles** *the Greek hero Hercules (see page 170)*

25–26 **tear a cat** rant and rave

31 **Phibbus' car** *the chariot of Phoebus, god of the sun (see page 170)*

35 **lofty** high-flown

36 **vein** style

45 **That's all one** that doesn't matter

46 **as small** with as high a voice

47 **An** if

48 **'Thisne …'** *Bottom's pronunciation of 'Thisby'*

   monstrous extraordinarily

BOTTOM	What is Pyramus, a lover or a tyrant?
QUINCE	A lover, that kills himself most gallant for love. 　20
BOTTOM	That will ask some tears in the true performing of it. If I do it, let the audience look to their eyes: I will move storms; I will condole in some measure. To the rest – yet my chief humour is for a tyrant. I could play Ercles rarely, or a part to tear 　25 a cat in, to make all split:

> The raging rocks
> And shivering shocks
> Shall break the locks
> Of prison-gates; 　　　　　　　　　　　30
> And Phibbus' car
> Shall shine from far,
> And make and mar
> The foolish Fates.

	This was lofty! Now name the rest of the players. 　35 This is Ercles' vein, a tyrant's vein: a lover is more condoling.
QUINCE	Francis Flute, the bellows-mender.
FLUTE	Here, Peter Quince.
QUINCE	Flute, you must take Thisby on you. 　　　　　40
FLUTE	What is Thisby, a wandering knight?
QUINCE	It is the lady that Pyramus must love.
FLUTE	Nay, faith, let not me play a woman; I have a beard coming.
QUINCE	That's all one; you shall play it in a mask, and you 　45 may speak as small as you will.
BOTTOM	An I may hide my face, let me play Thisby too: I'll speak in a monstrous little voice: 'Thisne, Thisne'. 'Ah Pyramus, my lover dear! thy Thisby dear, and lady dear!' 　　　　　　　　　　　　　　50
QUINCE	No, no, you must play Pyramus; and Flute, you Thisby.

1.2 Peter Quince's house

The other mechanicals are given their parts. As soon as Bottom hears that Snug is to play the lion, he wants to play that too, and Peter Quince has to convince him that he is ideal for Pyramus.

Activities

Character review: Bottom (1)

First impressions

Bottom might well get the vote as most people's favourite of all Shakespeare's characters, and actors greatly enjoy performing the part. What impression have you formed from his first appearance?

In groups of six, act out pages 17–21 and then list all the things you have discovered about Bottom. What have you learned, for example, from:

- his early suggestions to Peter Quince (lines 1–15)?
- his reaction to being given the part of Pyramus (lines 19–24)?
- the kind of acting he enjoys and his favourite parts (lines 24–37)?
- his offers to play Thisby (lines 47–50) and the lion (lines 66–79)?

Bottom (Des Barrit) and Quince (Philip Voss) in the 1994 Royal Shakespeare Theatre Company (RSC) production

61 **fitted** sorted out

63 **of study** at learning (*lines*)

64 **extempore** without preparing it beforehand

76 **discretion** sense

aggravate *Bottom means the opposite: I will make my voice softer.*

77 **roar you** 'roar for you'; *or simply:* roar

78 **sucking** unweaned; very young

an't were as though it were

81 **proper** handsome

BOTTOM	Well, proceed.	
QUINCE	Robin Starveling, the tailor.	
STARVELING	Here, Peter Quince.	55
QUINCE	Robin Starveling, you must play Thisby's mother. Tom Snout, the tinker.	
SNOUT	Here, Peter Quince.	
QUINCE	You, Pyramus' father; myself, Thisby's father; Snug the joiner, you, the lion's part: and I hope, here is a play fitted.	60
SNUG	Have you the lion's part written? Pray you, if it be, give it me, for I am slow of study.	
QUINCE	You may do it extempore, for it is nothing but roaring.	65
BOTTOM	Let me play the lion too; I will roar that I will do any man's heart good to hear me. I will roar, that I will make the Duke say, 'Let him roar again, let him roar again.'	
QUINCE	An you should do it too terribly, you would fright the Duchess and the ladies, that they would shriek; and that were enough to hang us all.	70
ALL	That would hang us, every mother's son.	
BOTTOM	I grant you, friends, if you should fright the ladies out of their wits, they would have no more discretion but to hang us; but I will aggravate my voice so, that I will roar you as gently as any sucking dove; I will roar you an 't were any nightingale.	75
QUINCE	You can play no part but Pyramus; for Pyramus is a sweet-faced man, a proper man as one shall see in a summer's day, a most lovely, gentleman-like-man; therefore you must needs play Pyramus.	80

1.2 Peter Quince's house

Bottom agrees to play Pyramus. They discuss what colour beard he should wear, and agree to meet the following night in the wood outside the city, so that they can rehearse in secret.

Activities

Character review: Peter Quince (1)

His plans for the play

In pairs, conduct an interview between a reporter from the *Athens Independent* and Peter Quince, for an article which will be headlined: 'New Play for Duke's Wedding'. Ask Quince:

- what the play is about and who the main characters are
- who will be performing in it and whether they have any theatrical experience
- what reactions there have so far been from the actors (are they excited, anxious, confident ...?)
- what impression they hope to make on the Duke and the court
- what issues they have so far discussed
- when and where they will rehearse (but see lines 97–99).

Actors' interpretations: '... hold or cut bow-strings.'

How would you say Bottom's exit line? In the 1999 RSC production, Daniel Ryan repeated the line in different voices and styles (as Sean Connery and Michael Cain, and then in a Robin Hood delivery). Decide what effect you want to achieve (humorous? dramatic?) and try saying it in different ways.

84 **What beard ... ?** *Bottom might be interested in woven false beards because of his trade. The colours he lists (lines 87–90) are all well-known dyes: orange-tawny = dark yellow; purple-in-grain = dyed with a fast purple or red; French-crown-coloured = pale yellow, like a gold coin.*

87 **discharge** perform

91–92 **Some of ... bare-faced** *Quince's joke is based on the fact that syphilis ('the French disease') caused baldness.*

Bare-faced (1) without a beard; (2) exposed without a disguise

94 **con** learn

96 **without** outside

98 **dogged** followed

99 **devices** plans

100 **bill of properties** list of props

103 **obscenely** *Bottom probably means 'unseen' (secretly).*

103–104 **be perfect** know your lines

104 **adieu** farewell (*French* à dieu = *to God*)

106 **hold or cut bow-strings** *Perhaps a reference to archers, who would cut the strings of their bows if they were running away, to render them useless to the enemy; it might mean: 'Keep your word, or be disgraced!'*

| BOTTOM | Well, I will undertake it. What beard were I best to play it in? | 85 |

| QUINCE | Why, what you will. | |

| BOTTOM | I will discharge it, in either your straw-colour beard, your orange-tawny beard, your purple-in-grain beard, or your French-crown-coloured beard, your perfect yellow. | 90 |

| QUINCE | Some of your French crowns have no hair at all, and then you will play bare-faced. But, masters, here are your parts, and I am to entreat you, request you, and desire you, to con them by tomorrow night; and meet me in the palace wood, a mile without the town, by moonlight. There will we rehearse: for if we meet in the city, we shall be dogged with company, and our devices known. In the meantime I will draw a bill of properties, such as our play wants. I pray you, fail me not. | 95 100 |

| BOTTOM | We will meet, and there we may rehearse most obscenely and courageously. Take pains; be perfect; adieu. | |

| QUINCE | At the Duke's oak we meet. | 105 |

| BOTTOM | Enough; hold or cut bow-strings. | |

Exeunt.

Exam practice

Character review: Helena (2)

What's in her mind?
In 1.1 Helena makes a bold decision. Imagine you are Helena. Write down your thoughts after you have decided to tell Demetrius about Hermia's planned flight with Lysander. You could begin: *This is risky ...*

Before you begin to write you should think about Helena's views on:
- her feelings about Demetrius
- her feelings about Hermia's beauty
- Demetrius's treatment of her and his love for Hermia
- what Helena hopes to gain by telling Demetrius of Hermia's planned elopement
- her attitude towards love.

Shakespeare's language: the mechanicals

Audiences often laugh at the mechanicals' language. In pairs, talk about the comic effect in 1.2 of:
- contradictions: lines 2–3 ('generally ... scrip'), line 7 ('wedding-day at night'), line 11 ('lamentable comedy')
- odd pronunciations: line 25 ('Ercles'), line 31 ('Phibbus'), line 48 ('Thisne')
- malapropisms (using a wrong word which sounds similar): line 76 ('aggravate'), line 103 ('obscenely')
- tautology (unnecessary repetition): lines 93–94 ('entreat ... request ... desire').

Character review: the mechanicals (2)

Their acting experience

A Do you think any of the mechanicals has been in a play before? Are any of them regular theatre-goers?
1. What do they say in 1.2 which suggests that:
   - Quince is basing Pyramus and Thisby on other plays that he has seen (lines 11–12; 45–46; 64–65)?
   - Bottom has some idea of 'stock characters' – familiar types to be found in popular drama, such as 'the lover' or 'the tyrant' (lines 19; 24–25)?
   - Bottom is impressed by over-the-top acting in very dramatic plays (lines 25–35)?
2. What does their discussion about the lion tell us (lines 70–79)?

B In most productions, the actors will try to distinguish the mechanicals, giving each one special characteristics. In pairs, make notes on the differences that you have noticed between the characters. Then fill in the following chart for each character. The first four lines can be completed by looking back at the script; the remaining points are for you to fill in either from a production that you have seen, or from clues about the characters to be found in the script, or simply from your own ideas. This example has been filled in for Peter Quince, as played by Peter Kelly in the 1999 RSC production:

24

FULL NAME: Peter Quince
TRADE: Carpenter
PART IN 'PYRAMUS AND THISBY' (according to the current decisions): Thisby's
father
ANY KNOWN DETAILS: is organising the play
AGE: 50
POSSIBLE PERSONALITY: pays attention to detail; generally patient but likes to
get his own way; controls the others
VOICE AND ACCENT: precise way of speaking; Edinburgh accent
MANNERISMS: fussy movements
APPEARANCE: long grey hair, tied at the back; quite formally dressed

C The best way in which to appreciate the mechanicals' humour and charm is to
act the scene out. Before you do so, look back at all the activities you have
completed so far and discuss your characters in groups of six. Make sure that
you bring out your own character's personality and mannerisms, and work
together to create a memorable scene. (If possible, learn a section of the scene:
this will enable you to perform it more convincingly – and enjoyably.)

Plot review (2): the lovers

To remind yourself about who loves whom and what problems they have,
re-read 1.1 and write a diary entry for each of the four lovers. Include:
- who they love
- what problems they are facing
- what their plans are.

Themes: love (4)

'The course of true love never did run smooth ...'
Write an answer to Helena's problem page letter (see page 12) in which the
agony aunt (or uncle) explains that love is never easy. Base your statements on
ideas from Act 1:
- Lysander's and Hermia's list of difficulties (1.1.132–140) and comments on the
  nature of love (lines 141–155)
- stories of lovers breaking vows (1.1.173–176)
- the situation on which 'Pyramus and Thisby' is based (1.2.20).

Shakespeare's language: mythology

Throughout *A Midsummer Night's Dream* there are many references drawn
from classical mythology. Look back through Act 1 to see how the following
classical names are used, checking the references with the background details
on pages 170–171:
- *places and characters*: Athens, Theseus, Hippolyta
- *gods and goddesses*: Diana (1.1.89), Cupid and Venus (1.1.169 and 235),
  Phoebe (1.1.209), Phoebus (1.2.31)
- *figures from classical myths and legends*: Dido and Aeneas (1.1.173), Hercules
  (1.2.25).

Start to keep a list of these classical references, under the three headings, in
preparation for a later activity.

2.1 A wood near Athens

In the wood a fairy encounters Robin Goodfellow, also known as Puck, henchman to Oberon, King of the fairies. Puck warns the fairy that Oberon is on his way, angry because his queen, Titania, is refusing to hand over an Indian boy. There have been repeated conflicts between them.

Activities

Character review: Puck (1)

What is he like?
What impression do you receive of Puck from each of the production photographs on this page and page 28?

Barry Lynch as Puck (RSC 1994)

Richard McCabe as Puck (RSC 1989)

3 **Thorough** through

4 **pale** fenced in land

7 **moonés sphere** moon's orbit (*People believed that the moon, planets and stars were fixed in transparent spheres circling the earth – see line 153.*)

9 **orbs** circles (*'fairy rings'*)

10 **pensioners** royal bodyguard

12 **favours** marks of royal favour; the Queen's gifts

13 **savours** fragrance

16 **thou lob of spirits** you lout among fairies

20 **passing fell and wrath** extremely fierce and angry

23 **changeling** *It was believed that fairies stole human babies and left fairy children in their place; here 'changeling' refers to the stolen child.*

25 **trace** range through

26 **perforce withholds** keeps him by force

29 **spangled ... sheen** bright, glittering starlight

30 **square** quarrel

33 **shrewd and knavish** mischievous and roguish

35 **villagery** local villages

36 **Skim milk** steal the cream off the milk

labour in the quern work to mess up the corn-grinding

Act 2

Scene 1

A wood near Athens.

Enter a Fairy *at one side, and* PUCK *at another.*

PUCK   How now, spirit, whither wander you?

FAIRY   Over hill, over dale,
Thorough bush, thorough brier,
Over park, over pale,
Thorough flood, thorough fire;   5
I do wander everywhere,
Swifter than the moonés sphere;
And I serve the Fairy Queen,
To dew her orbs upon the green.
The cowslips tall her pensioners be;   10
In their gold coats spots you see,
Those be rubies, fairy favours,
In those freckles live their savours.
I must go seek some dew-drops here,
And hang a pearl in every cowslip's ear.   15
Farewell, thou lob of spirits; I'll be gone;
Our Queen and all her elves come here anon.

PUCK   The King doth keep his revels here tonight;
Take heed the Queen come not within his sight;
For Oberon is passing fell and wrath,   20
Because that she as her attendant hath
A lovely boy stolen from an Indian King;
She never had so sweet a changeling.
And jealous Oberon would have the child
Knight of his train, to trace the forests wild; 25
But she perforce witholds the lovéd boy,
Crowns him with flowers, and makes him all her joy.
And now they never meet in grove or green,
By fountain clear, or spangled starlight sheen,
But they do square, that all their elves for fear 30
Creep into acorn cups and hide them there.

FAIRY   Either I mistake your shape and making quite,
Or else you are that shrewd and knavish sprite
Called Robin Goodfellow. Are not you he,
That frights the maidens of the villagery,   35
Skim milk, and sometimes labour in the quern,

27

2.1 A wood near Athens

The fairy tells Puck what she has heard about him, and he gleefully describes some of his mischief-making. Suddenly Oberon and Titania arrive and confront one another.

Activities

Character review: Puck (2)

A wanted poster
Use the Fairy's accusations (lines 32–42) and Puck's own admissions (lines 42–58) to create a 'Wanted' poster for Puck. It might include:

- a picture (based upon one of the images on this page or page 26)
- information about his various disguises (lines 46, 48 and 52)
- a list of the deeds he is wanted for (lines 35–39 and 47–54)
- the places he has been known to frequent
- the names of his known associates (line 44)
- a record of his various names (lines 34 and 40).

Leonard Preston as Puck (RSC 1977)

37 **bootless** in vain (*She churns, but the butter will not form.*)

38 **barm** froth on the ale (*The yeast won't ferment, or the beer is flat.*)

39 **Mislead** lead out of their way

41 **You do their work** *Another belief was that Puck would do housework at night if treated politely.*

45 **beguile** deceive

47 **gossip's** old woman's

48 **crab** crab-apple

50 **dewlap** loose flesh around her throat

51 **aunt** old woman

   saddest most serious

54 **'tailor'** *There was a custom of crying 'tailor' if you fell backwards off a stool; 'tail' could also mean 'bum' (line 53).*

55 **quire** company

56 **waxen ... neeze** laugh even more and sneeze (*or perhaps: snort*)

62 **forsworn** sworn to avoid

63 **wanton** rebellious person

66 **Corin ... Phillida** *proverbial names for a shepherd and his lover*

69 **steep** mountainside

And bootless make the breathless housewife churn,
And sometimes make the drink to bear no barm,
Mislead night-wanderers, laughing at their harm?
Those that Hobgoblin call you, and sweet Puck,   40
You do their work, and they shall have good luck.
Are not you he?

PUCK   Thou speak'st aright;
I am that merry wanderer of the night.
I jest to Oberon, and make him smile,
When I a fat and bean-fed horse beguile,   45
Neighing in likeness of a filly foal;
And sometimes lurk I in a gossip's bowl,
In very likeness of a roasted crab;
And when she drinks, against her lips I bob,
And on her withered dewlap pour the ale.   50
The wisest aunt, telling the saddest tale,
Sometime for three-foot stool mistaketh me;
Then slip I from her bum, down topples she,
And 'tailor' cries, and falls into a cough;
And then the whole quire hold their hips, and
     laugh,   55
And waxen in their mirth, and neeze, and swear
A merrier hour was never wasted there.
But room, fairy! here comes Oberon.

FAIRY   And here my mistress! Would that he were gone!

Enter OBERON King of the Fairies at one side with his train, and TITANIA the Queen at another with hers.

OBERON   Ill met by moonlight, proud Titania.   60

TITANIA   What, jealous Oberon? Fairies, skip hence:
            I have forsworn his bed and company.

OBERON   Tarry, rash wanton; am not I thy lord?

TITANIA   Then I must be thy lady; but I know
            When thou hast stolen away from fairy land,   65
            And in the shape of Corin sat all day,
            Playing on pipes of corn, and versing love
            To amorous Phillida. Why art thou here,
            Come from the farthest steep of India,

2.1 A wood near Athens

When Titania challenges Oberon about his affection for Hippolyta, he retaliates by accusing her of favouring Theseus. Titania complains that Oberon has repeatedly ruined her fairies' dances and has disturbed the natural pattern of the seasons.

Activities

Actors' interpretations: the fairy world

Act 1 took place in Athens, among courtiers and ordinary working men. What would you do if you were asked to design a production of this play, in order to show that the scene has changed to the fairy world of the wood? Draw sketches and make notes to show how this new world might be represented through:

- costumes (style, colours, fabrics …)
- set
- music and other sound effects
- the fairies' appearance (skin colour, hair, make-up …)
- the actions and movements of the fairies (like insects, small mammals, children …).

70 **forsooth** indeed

bouncing athletic

71 **buskined** wearing hunting boots

75 **Glance at my credit** jibe at my relationship

78–80 **Peregenia … Antiopa** *Theseus had had sexual relations with all these women.*

85 **beached margent** shore

86 **ringlets** circular dances

90 **Contagious** carrying disease

91 **pelting** paltry, insignificant

92 **overborne their continents** broken their banks

95 **ere** before

97 **murrion** infected with murrain (*a disease*)

98 **nine men's morris** *area of ground marked out for a game*

99 **quaint mazes** intricate systems of paths

wanton green luxuriant grass

101 **want** lack

103 **Therefore** That is why

governess *because it controls the tides*

105 **That** so that

rheumatic diseases *ailments such as colds and coughs*

106 **distemperature** (1) bad weather; (2) disorder

109 **Hiems** winter (*personified*)

2.1

	But that, forsooth, the bouncing Amazon,	70
	Your buskined mistress, and your warrior love,
	To Theseus must be wedded; and you come
	To give their bed joy and prosperity.

OBERON   How canst thou thus, for shame, Titania,
Glance at my credit with Hippolyta,   75
Knowing I know thy love to Theseus?
Didst thou not lead him through the glimmering
    night
From Peregenia, whom he ravishéd?
And make him with fair Aegles break his faith,
With Ariadne, and Antiopa?   80

TITANIA   These are the forgeries of jealousy;
And never since the middle summer's spring
Met we on hill, in dale, forest, or mead,
By pavéd fountain, or by rushy brook,
Or in the beachéd margent of the sea,   85
To dance our ringlets to the whistling wind,
But with thy brawls thou hast disturbed our sport.
Therefore the winds, piping to us in vain,
As in revenge have sucked up from the sea
Contagious fogs; which, falling in the land,   90
Have every pelting river made so proud
That they have overborne their continents.
The ox hath therefore stretched his yoke in vain,
The ploughman lost his sweat, and the green corn
Hath rotted ere his youth attained a beard: 95
The fold stands empty in the drownéd field,
And crows are fatted with the murrion flock;
The nine men's morris is filled up with mud,
And the quaint mazes in the wanton green,
For lack of tread, are undistinguishable.   100
The human mortals want their winter cheer;
No night is now with hymn or carol blest;
Therefore the moon, the governess of floods,
Pale in her anger, washes all the air,
That rheumatic diseases do abound.   105
And thorough this distemperature we see
The seasons alter; hoary-headed frosts
Fall in the fresh lap of the crimson rose,
And on old Hiems' thin and icy crown

2.1 A wood near Athens

Oberon offers to end the conflict if Titania will give him the 'changeling boy'. But she refuses, explaining that his mother had been one of her worshippers, and had died giving birth.

Activities

Themes: order and disorder (1)

'The seasons alter ...'

A In pairs, re-read lines 60–145 and check that you know:
- why Oberon and Titania are in conflict (lines 118–121)
- how long the dispute has been going on (line 82)
- what effect it has had upon the natural world (lines 88–114)
- why Titania refuses to agree to Oberon's demands (lines 121–137).

B 1. Which single word in Titania's speech (lines 81–117) shows that the disturbances in nature have happened *as a result* of their dispute?
  2. Find the sections of Titania's speech which suggest that:
  - their dispute has been going on since early summer
  - rivers have broken their banks
  - crops have been blighted
  - sheep have drowned in the floods
  - woodland paths are covered in mud
  - the damp, unhealthy weather has caused illness
  - the seasons have become mixed up.

continued on page 34

110 **odorous chaplet** sweet-smelling garland

112 **childing** fruitful

113 **wonted liveries** customary uniforms (usual colours)

mazéd amazed

114 **their increase** the products of the different seasons

115 **progeny** offspring

116 **debate** quarrel

117 **original** origin

118 **amend it** put it right

121 **henchman** page of honour, squire

123 **votaress** *woman who had taken a vow to worship Titania in her sisterhood* (**order**)

126 **Neptune** *Roman god of the sea (see page 170)*

127 **embarkéd ... flood** merchant ships at sea

128–129 **conceive ... wind** *the sails seem to become pregnant by the sexually irresponsible (***wanton***) wind*

130 **gait** movement

133 **trifles** little presents

135 **of** giving birth to

139 **Perchance** perhaps

140 **round** round dance

142 **spare** avoid

145 **chide downright** quarrel openly

An odorous chaplet of sweet summer buds 110
Is, as in mockery, set. The spring, the summer,
The childing autumn, angry winter, change
Their wonted liveries, and the mazéd world,
By their increase, now knows not which is which.
And this same progeny of evils comes 115
From our debate, from our dissension;
We are their parents and original.

OBERON Do you amend it, then; it lies in you.
Why should Titania cross her Oberon?
I do but beg a little changeling boy 120
To be my henchman.

TITANIA   Set your heart at rest;
The fairy land buys not the child of me.
His mother was a votaress of my order,
And in the spicéd Indian air, by night,
Full often hath she gossiped by my side; 125
And sat with me on Neptune's yellow sands,
Marking th' embarkéd traders on the flood;
When we have laughed to see the sails conceive,
And grow big-bellied with the wanton wind;
Which she with pretty and with swimming gait 130
Following, her womb then rich with my young
   squire,
Would imitate, and sail upon the land
To fetch me trifles; and return again,
As from a voyage, rich with merchandise.
But she, being mortal, of that boy did die; 135
And for her sake do I rear up her boy,
And for her sake I will not part with him.

OBERON How long within this wood intend you stay?

TITANIA Perchance till after Theseus' wedding-day.
If you will patiently dance in our round, 140
And see our moonlight revels, go with us;
If not, shun me, and I will spare your haunts.

OBERON Give me that boy, and I will go with thee.

TITANIA Not for thy fairy kingdom. Fairies, away:
We shall chide downright, if I longer stay. 145

2.1 A wood near Athens

When Titania leaves, Oberon plans his revenge. He recalls a time when he saw a flower hit by Cupid's arrow and tells Puck to fetch it for him. The juice of the flower (called 'love-in-idleness') has the power to make someone fall in love with the first thing they see, and Oberon plans to use it on Titania.

Activities

3. How much sympathy do you have for Titania and her reasons for not giving up the boy (lines 123–137)?

C In many of Shakespeare's plays, disturbances among rulers are often paralleled by disturbances in nature. People seemed terrified about the consequences of civil disorder, and feared a repetition of the Wars of the Roses in the fifteenth century.

Write the version of Titania's speech (lines 88–114) that Shakespeare might have composed if he were alive today. Find images of war, starvation and ecological disasters to illustrate your text. (If you are feeling confident, you might write in blank verse – see pages 171–174.)

Nicholas Jones as Oberon and Josette Simon as Titania (RSC 1999)

149 **Since** the time when

151 **dulcet ... breath** sweet ... song

152 **rude** (1) rough; (2) ill-mannered

civil (1) gentle; (2) polite

153 **spheres** *see line 7*

157 **certain** sure

158 **fair vestal ... west** beautiful virgin queen in the west (*see line 163*)

159 **love-shaft** golden arrow of love (*see 1.1.169*); *the person it hit would fall in love*

161 **might** could

162 **chaste** sexually pure (*the fiery arrow was extinguished when it hit the moon's reflection in the water*)

163 **vot'ress** *The queen worshipped Diana, goddess of the moon and virgins; these lines possible refer to Elizabeth I – the 'virgin Queen'.*

165 **bolt** arrow

168 **Love-in-idleness** pansy, or heartsease

171 **or ... or** either ... or

dote be infatuated with

174 **leviathan** *mythical sea-monster (and the Elizabethans' term for the whale)*

OBERON　Well, go thy way; thou shalt not from this grove,
　　　　Till I torment thee for this injury.
　　　　My gentle Puck, come hither. Thou rememb'rest
　　　　Since once I sat upon a promontory,
　　　　And heard a mermaid on a dolphin's back　　　150
　　　　Uttering such dulcet and harmonious breath
　　　　That the rude sea grew civil at her song,
　　　　And certain stars shot madly from their spheres
　　　　To hear the sea-maid's music.

PUCK　　　　　　　　　　　　I remember.

OBERON　That very time I saw, but thou couldst not,　　155
　　　　Flying between the cold moon and the earth,
　　　　Cupid, all armed; a certain aim he took
　　　　At a fair vestal thronéd by the west,
　　　　And loosed his love-shaft smartly from his bow
　　　　As it should pierce a hundred thousand hearts;　160
　　　　But I might see young Cupid's fiery shaft
　　　　Quenched in the chaste beams of the watery moon;
　　　　And the imperial vot'ress passéd on,
　　　　In maiden meditation, fancy-free.
　　　　Yet marked I where the bolt of Cupid fell:　　165
　　　　It fell upon a little western flower;
　　　　Before, milk-white, now purple with love's wound,
　　　　And maidens call it Love-in-idleness.
　　　　Fetch me that flower, the herb I shewed thee once.
　　　　The juice of it on sleeping eye-lids laid　　　170
　　　　Will make or man or woman madly dote
　　　　Upon the next live creature that it sees.
　　　　Fetch me this herb, and be thou here again
　　　　Ere the leviathan can swim a league.

PUCK　　I'll put a girdle round about the earth　　　175
　　　　In forty minutes.

Exit PUCK.

OBERON　　　　　　　　　Having once this juice,
　　　　I'll watch Titania when she is asleep,
　　　　And drop the liquor of it in her eyes:
　　　　The next thing then she waking looks upon,

2.1 A wood near Athens

Oberon plans to anoint Titania's eyelids with the juice as she sleeps: when she wakes, and is distracted by falling in love with some hideous creature, he will get the child from her. Hearing people approaching, Oberon makes himself invisible and overhears Demetrius rejecting Helena.

Activities

Actors' interpretations: *Enter Demetrius, Helena following him*

The actors playing Helena and Demetrius have to enter at 2.1.187 in the middle of a heated exchange and will have thought in rehearsals about what has happened before they come on stage.

1. In pairs, re-read Helena's plan from Act 1 (1.1.246–251). Then improvise a scene in which Helena catches up with Demetrius in the wood: she explains why she revealed Lysander's and Hermia's secret (1.1.157–168 and 209–219) and he angrily rejects her.
2. What exactly is Demetrius implying in his threats to Helena (2.1.214–219 and 235–237)? Should we take his threats seriously?

182 **soul** very essence

185 **render** give

187 **conference** conversation

190 **slayeth me** kills me (*for love of her*)

192 **wood** mad

195 **adamant** *hard magnetic stone which can attract (***draw**, *lines 196–197) metal*

199 **entice … speak you fair** try to attract you … say nice things to you

203 **spaniel** *famous for its faithfulness*

211 **Tempt … spirit** don't push my hatred of you too far

214 **impeach your modesty** risk harming your sexual reputation

2.1

Be it on lion, bear, or wolf, or bull,   180
On meddling monkey, or on busy ape,
She shall pursue it with the soul of love.
And ere I take this charm from off her sight,
As I can take it with another herb,
I'll make her render up her page to me.   185
But who comes here? I am invisible,
And I will overhear their conference.

Enter DEMETRIUS, HELENA *following him.*

DEMETRIUS	I love thee not, therefore pursue me not.
	Where is Lysander, and fair Hermia?
	The one I'll slay, the other slayeth me. 190
	Thou told'st me they were stolen unto this wood;
	And here am I, and wood within this wood,
	Because I cannot meet my Hermia.
	Hence, get thee gone, and follow me no more!
HELENA	You draw me, you hard-hearted adamant, 195
	But yet you draw not iron, for my heart
	Is true as steel. Leave you your power to draw,
	And I shall have no power to follow you.
DEMETRIUS	Do I entice you? Do I speak you fair?
	Or rather do I not in plainest truth 200
	Tell you I do not nor I cannot love you?
HELENA	And even for that do I love you the more.
	I am your spaniel; and, Demetrius,
	The more you beat me, I will fawn on you.
	Use me but as your spaniel; spurn me, strike me, 205
	Neglect me, lose me; only give me leave,
	Unworthy as I am, to follow you.
	What worser place can I beg in your love,
	And yet a place of high respect with me,
	Than to be uséd as you use your dog? 210
DEMETRIUS	Tempt not too much the hatred of my spirit;
	For I am sick when I do look on thee.
HELENA	And I am sick when I look not on you.
DEMETRIUS	You do impeach your modesty too much,

2.1 A wood near Athens

Watching Demetrius cruelly spurning Helena and running away from her, Oberon vows that he will turn the tables, so that Demetrius ends up pursuing her.

Activities

Actors' interpretations: 'I am invisible'

Oberon sometimes gets a laugh from the audience when he informs them in a matter-of-fact way 'I am invisible' (line 186). But the point is, he only has to say this for us to accept the fact. This is because, unlike the mechanicals, we know the rules of theatre and know how easy it is to make the audience believe in something if it is done simply and with confidence.

Having become invisible, what does Oberon actually do during the exchange between Helena and Demetrius (lines 187–244)? Is it most effective if he:

- stands silently at the back of the stage?
- walks around, reacting to what they say?
- magically influences their behaviour in some way?

In groups of three, act out the scene in each of these different ways and decide which one you prefer, talking about the advantages and disadvantages of each approach.

---

215 **To leave** by leaving

218 **ill counsel … desert place** the wicked thoughts inspired by being alone in a deserted spot

220 **Your virtue …** your special qualities protect me; because **(for that) …**

224 **in my respect** to my mind

227 **brakes** thickets

230–231 **the story shall be changed** *In the original myth, Daphne was turned into a laurel tree to escape being caught by the god Apollo. (See page 170)*

232 **griffin** *a monster with the body of a lion, and the head and wings of an eagle*

bootless useless, pointless *(see 2.1.37)*

235 **stay** wait to hear

236–237 **do not believe But** … you'd better believe that

237 **mischief** harm

239 **Fie** *a common expression of disapproval*

240 **Your wrongs … sex** the wrongs you do me cause me to behave in a way that disgraces women

244 **upon** by

	To leave the city and commit yourself	215
	Into the hands of one that loves you not;
	To trust the opportunity of night
	And the ill counsel of a desert place
	With the rich worth of your virginity.

HELENA   Your virtue is my privilege: for that   220
          It is not night when I do see your face,
          Therefore I think I am not in the night;
          Nor doth this wood lack worlds of company,
          For you, in my respect, are all the world.
          Then how can it be said I am alone,   225
          When all the world is here to look on me?

DEMETRIUS I'll run from thee and hide me in the brakes,
          And leave thee to the mercy of wild beasts.

HELENA   The wildest hath not such a heart as you.
          Run when you will, the story shall be changed: 230
          Apollo flies, and Daphne holds the chase;
          The dove pursues the griffin, the mild hind
          Makes speed to catch the tiger; bootless speed,
          When cowardice pursues, and valour flies.

DEMETRIUS I will not stay thy questions; let me go;   235
          Or, if thou follow me, do not believe
          But I shall do thee mischief in the wood.

HELENA   Ay, in the temple, in the town, the field
          You do me mischief. Fie, Demetrius;
          Your wrongs do set a scandal on my sex: 240
          We cannot fight for love, as men may do;
          We should be wooed, and were not made to woo.

Exit DEMETRIUS.

          I'll follow thee, and make a heaven of hell,
          To die upon the hand I love so well.

Exit HELENA.

OBERON   Fare thee well, nymph; ere he do leave this grove, 245
          Thou shalt fly him, and he shall seek thy love.

Re-enter PUCK.

2.2 The wood

Oberon first explains how he plans to anoint Titania's eyes with the juice, and then tells him to find the young man who is spurning 'a sweet Athenian lady'. Puck is to anoint Demetrius's eyes so that he will fall in love with Helena when he awakes. Elsewhere, Titania and her fairies arrive at her usual sleeping-place.

Activities

Character review: Oberon (1)

Oberon's feelings

Oberon's speech 'I know a bank ...' (lines 249–258) is often quoted by people as a rather romantic piece of poetry about the beauties of nature; but there is no reason why it has to be delivered like that. In fact, the tone of the speech will depend upon the mood of the Oberon speaking it.

- What is your impression of Oberon at this point in the play?
- How exactly does he want to use the magic flower on Titania?
- What does he hope will come of it?
- Does his planned action strike you as an amusing practical joke or spiteful revenge?

When you have answered these questions, perform the speech in several different ways:

- light-heartedly, as though very fond of Titania
- maliciously, as though wanting revenge
- humorously, as though enjoying the practical joke
- any other ways you can think of.

Decide which interpretation fits your view of Oberon.

249 **blows** blooms

251–252 **over-canopied ... eglantine** roofed over with luxurious honeysuckle, rambling roses and sweet-briar

253 **sometime** for some part of

256 **Weed wide enough** making a garment which is wide enough

258 **hateful fantasies** horrible delusions

266 **fond on** infatuated with

267 **look** make sure

1 **roundel** round dance

3 **cankers** maggots and caterpillars

4 **rere-mice** bats

6 **clamorous** noisy

7 **quaint** dainty

8 **offices** jobs (*listed in lines 3–7*)

40

Hast thou the flower there? Welcome, wanderer.

PUCK   Ay, there it is.

OBERON   I pray thee give it me.
I know a bank whereon the wild thyme blows;
Where oxlips and the nodding violet grows,   250
Quite over-canopied with luscious woodbine,
With sweet musk-roses, and with eglantine;
There sleeps Titania sometime of the night,
Lulled in those flowers with dances and delight;
And there the snake throws her enamelled skin,   255
Weed wide enough to wrap a fairy in;
And with the juice of this I'll streak her eyes,
And make her full of hateful fantasies.
Take thou some of it, and seek through this grove:
A sweet Athenian lady is in love   260
With a disdainful youth: anoint his eyes;
But do it when the next thing he espies
May be the lady. Thou shalt know the man
By the Athenian garments he hath on.
Effect it with some care, that he may prove   265
More fond on her than she upon her love;
And look thou meet me ere the first cock crow.

PUCK   Fear not, my lord; your servant shall do so.

Exeunt.

Scene 2

The wood, with TITANIA's *sleeping-place behind.*

Enter TITANIA, *with her train.*

TITANIA   Come now, a roundel, and a fairy song;
Then, for the third part of a minute, hence;
Some to kill cankers in the musk-rose buds.
Some war with rere-mice for their leathern wings,
To make my small elves coats, and some keep back   5
The clamorous owl that nightly hoots and wonders
At our quaint spirits. Sing me now asleep;
Then to your offices, and let me rest.

2.2 The wood

Titania falls asleep after the fairies have sung a lullaby and Oberon enters to squeeze the magic juice on to her eyes. As he leaves, Lysander and Hermia arrive on the scene, exhausted and lost.

Shakespeare's language: magic spells

Oberon's spell (lines 26–33) is in a different verse form from his usual speeches: it has four main stresses (rather than five) and rhymes in couplets. (The same verse form, known as 'trochaic', is used by other fairy characters at various moments in the play.)

Write your own magic spell in the same verse form.

Actors' interpretations: Oberon's afterthought

In some productions, Oberon seems to have completed his spell on line 32 ('When thou wak'st, it is thy dear.'); he walks away, then stops – as though he has thought of something extra to say – and then turns back to Titania, to add, as a special afterthought: 'Wake when some vile thing is near.'

Try acting it like this, and then act it again without the pause. What effect is achieved in each case? Which do you prefer?

11 **blind-worms** slow-worms (*Like newts, they were thought to be harmful – see* Macbeth, *4.1.14–16.*)

13 **Philomel** the nightingale

22 **offence** harm

25 **one aloof … sentinel** one fairy stand guard at a distance

28 **languish** lose all vitality through love

29 **ounce** lynx

30 **Pard** leopard

The Fairies *sing.*

FIRST FAIRY	*You spotted snakes with double tongue,*	
	Thorny hedgehogs, be not seen;	10
	Newts and blind-worms, do no wrong;	
	Come not near our Fairy Queen.	

CHORUS *Philomel with melody*
Sing in our sweet lullaby;
Lulla, lulla, lullaby, lulla, lulla, lullaby.   15
Never harm, nor spell, nor charm,
Come our lovely Lady nigh.
So good night, with lullaby.

SECOND *Weaving spiders, come not here,*
FAIRY *Hence, you long-legg'd spinners, hence;*   20
Beetles black, approach not near;
Worm nor snail do no offence.

CHORUS *Philomel with melody, etc.*

TITANIA *sleeps.*

FIRST FAIRY Hence away; now all is well;
One aloof stand sentinel.   25

Exeunt Fairies.

Enter OBERON, *who puts the juice on* TITANIA's *eyelids.*

OBERON What thou seest when thou dost wake,
Do it for thy true love take:
Love and languish for his sake.
Be it ounce, or cat, or bear,
Pard, or boar with bristled hair,   30
In thy eye that shall appear,
When thou wak'st, it is thy dear.
Wake when some vile thing is near.

Exit.

Enter LYSANDER *and* HERMIA.

LYSANDER Fair love, you faint with wandering in the wood,
And to speak truth, I have forgot our way.   35

2.2 The wood

Hermia and Lysander decide to stay where they are for the night. As they fall asleep, some way apart, Puck enters. He has so far not been able to find the couple that Oberon told him to look for; but suddenly spots Hermia and Lysander asleep.

Activities

Themes: love (5)

'Lie further off ...'

Lysander seems to want rather more physical contact than Hermia is happy with! Re-read their discussion about where to sleep (lines 38–64), make rough notes on each person's arguments, and then improvise the scene, referring to your notes if you have to.

Then go back to the script and jot down what you think each character is actually thinking (but not saying aloud) at key points in the exchange.

For example, you might start with lines 38–39, with Hermia thinking: 'I don't think it would be right to sleep next to him.'

Actors' interpretations: Lysander's reaction

How does the discussion between Lysander and Hermia end? What kind of a mood is Lysander in? Try saying his lines (lines 61–63) in different ways, for example:
- cheerfully agreeing with her argument
- bad-tempered because he hasn't got his way
- reluctantly accepting what she has said.

41 **one troth** one (shared) promise, or truth (*see lines 48–49*)

44 **O take ... innocence** O, don't misunderstand my innocent suggestion

45 **Love ... conference** in lovers' conversations, we should be able to understand one another

48 **bosoms** sets of feelings

51 **lie** (1) deceive you; (2) lie down

53 **much beshrew ...** a real curse on ...

58 **Becomes** is fitting for

67 **approve** test

	We'll rest us, Hermia, if you think it good, And tarry for the comfort of the day.	
HERMIA	Be it so, Lysander; find you out a bed, For I upon this bank will rest my head.	
LYSANDER	One turf shall serve as pillow for us both; One heart, one bed, two bosoms, and one troth.	40
HERMIA	Nay, good Lysander; for my sake, my dear, Lie further off yet, do not lie so near.	
LYSANDER	O take the sense, sweet, of my innocence. Love takes the meaning in love's conference. I mean that my heart unto yours is knit, So that but one heart we can make of it. Two bosoms interchainéd with an oath, So then, two bosoms, and a single troth. Then by your side no bed-room me deny, For lying so, Hermia, I do not lie.	45 50
HERMIA	Lysander riddles very prettily; Now much beshrew my manners and my pride, If Hermia meant to say Lysander lied. But, gentle friend, for love and courtesy Lie further off, in human modesty; Such separation as may well be said Becomes a virtuous bachelor and a maid; So far be distant, and good night, sweet friend: Thy love ne'er alter, till thy sweet life end!	 55 60
LYSANDER	Amen, amen, to that fair prayer say I; And then, end life, when I end loyalty! Here is my bed; sleep give thee all his rest.	
HERMIA	With half that wish, the wisher's eyes be pressed!	

They sleep. Enter PUCK.

PUCK	Through the forest have I gone, But Athenian found I none On whose eyes I might approve This flower's force in stirring love. Night and silence: who is here? Weeds of Athens he doth wear:	65 70

2.2 **The wood**

Noticing Lysander's Athenian clothes, Puck assumes that this is the couple he has been told to find, and he anoints Lysander's eyes as he sleeps. As Puck leaves, in comes Demetrius, pursued by Helena. Demetrius runs off and Helena, too tired to give chase, stumbles across the sleeping Lysander.

Activities

Plot review (3): who loves whom?

With the entrance of Puck, carrying the love-in-idleness (line 65), this is a good time to remind yourself about who loves whom. Draw Cupid's arrows in the diagram below to show the lovers' relationships as they have been since the opening of the play. (If Jack loves Jill, but Jill doesn't love Jack, the arrow would look like this: JACK → JILL. If they love each other, the arrow is pointed at both ends, like this: JACK ↔ JILL.)

Who loves whom: Phase 1 (up to 2.2.76)

HERMIA   LYSANDER

HELENA   DEMETRIUS

Copy the diagram and then draw up a Phase 2 version next to it (after Puck has anointed Lysander's eyes by mistake: from 2.2.77), showing any changes in a different colour.

75	**durst** dares
77	**Churl** heartless, ill-mannered person
78	**owe** possess (own)
79–80	**forbid … seat** prevent sleep from taking hold
84	**haunt** hang around
85	**darkling** in the dark
87	**fond** foolish
88	**the lesser … grace** the less my prayers are answered
95	**no marvel though** it's no wonder that
97	**dissembling** deceitful
98	**sphery eyne** starry eyes (*like stars which belong in the spheres – see 2.1.7*)

This is he, my master said,
Despiséd the Athenian maid:
And here the maiden, sleeping sound,
On the dank and dirty ground.
Pretty soul, she durst not lie   75
Near this lack-love, this kill-courtesy.
Churl, upon thy eyes I throw
All the power this charm doth owe:
When thou wak'st let love forbid
Sleep his seat on thy eyelid.   80
So awake when I am gone;
For I must now to Oberon.

Exit.

Enter DEMETRIUS *and* HELENA, *running.*

HELENA   Stay, though thou kill me, sweet Demetrius.

DEMETRIUS   I charge thee hence, and do not haunt me thus.

HELENA   O wilt thou darkling leave me? Do not so.   85

DEMETRIUS   Stay on thy peril; I alone will go.

Exit DEMETRIUS.

HELENA   O, I am out of breath, in this fond chase,
            The more my prayer, the lesser is my grace.
            Happy is Hermia, wheresoe'er she lies,
            For she hath blesséd and attractive eyes.   90
            How came her eyes so bright? Not with salt tears:
            If so, my eyes are oftener washed than hers.
            No, no, I am as ugly as a bear;
            For beasts that meet me run away for fear.
            Therefore no marvel though Demetrius   95
            Do as a monster, fly my presence thus.
            What wicked and dissembling glass of mine
            Made me compare with Hermia's sphery eyne?
            But who is here? Lysander on the ground!
            Dead or asleep? I see no blood, no wound.   100
            Lysander, if you live, good sir, awake!

2.2 The wood

Helena awakes Lysander and he, under the effects of the magic juice, immediately falls in love with her and tells her so. Thinking that he is making fun of her, Helena runs off.

Activities

Character review: Helena (3)

Her feelings
Re-read lines 87–133. Then in small groups, hot-seat Helena, asking her questions such as:

- How do you feel about Hermia?
- What image do you have of yourself?
- How do you account for Demetrius's rejection of you?
- What do you make of Lysander's declaration of love?
- What questions would you like to find the answers to?

Haydn Gwynne as Helena in the RSC 1994 production

103 **Transparent** (1) bright; (2) open, without deceit

art a magic power

108 **What though** what if

113 **raven ... dove** *These words suggest that Hermia is dark and Helena fair.*

114 **The will ... swayed** Our emotions are ruled by reason

117–119 **So I ... will** *Lysander argues that, until now, his powers of reasoning had not been fully developed; now that he has reached the peak of his intelligence (***point of human skill***), reason begins to rule his passions (***will***).*

120 **o'erlook** read (look over)

122 **Wherefore** why

127 **flout my insufficiency** mock my shortcomings, my inadequacy

128 **Good troth ... good sooth** *expressions meaning 'truly'*

130–131 **Perforce ... gentleness** I have to say, I thought you were more of a gentleman

133 **of** by

136–137 **as ... brings** just as eating too many sweets can put you off them completely

LYSANDER (*awaking*)
And run through fire I will for thy sweet sake!
Transparent Helena! Nature shows art,
That through thy bosom makes me see thy heart.
Where is Demetrius? O how fit a word   105
Is that vile name, to perish on my sword!

HELENA Do not say so, Lysander; say not so:
What though he love your Hermia? Lord, what
    though?
Yet Hermia still loves you; then be content.

LYSANDER Content with Hermia? No, I do repent   110
The tedious minutes I with her have spent.
Not Hermia but Helena I love:
Who will not change a raven for a dove?
The will of man is by his reason swayed;
And reason says you are the worthier maid.   115
Things growing are not ripe until their season;
So I, being young, till now ripe not to reason;
And touching now the point of human skill,
Reason becomes the marshal to my will,
And leads me to your eyes, where I o'erlook   120
Love's stories, written in love's richest book.

HELENA Wherefore was I to this keen mockery born?
When at your hands did I deserve this scorn?
Is 't not enough, is 't not enough, young man,
That I did never, no, nor never can   125
Deserve a sweet look from Demetrius' eye,
But you must flout my insufficiency?
Good troth, you do me wrong, good sooth, you do,
In such disdainful manner me to woo.
But fare you well; perforce I must confess   130
I thought you lord of more true gentleness.
O, that a lady of one man refused
Should of another therefore be abused!

Exit.

LYSANDER She sees not Hermia. Hermia, sleep thou there;
And never mayst thou come Lysander near.   135
For, as a surfeit of the sweetest things
The deepest loathing to the stomach brings,

2.2 The wood

Lysander says farewell to the sleeping Hermia and goes off to devote himself to the pursuit of Helena. Awaking from a frightening nightmare, only to find Lysander gone, Hermia runs off into the woods to find him.

Activities

Actors' interpretations: Lysander under the spell

Write director's notes to lines 87–143, helping the actors playing Helena and Lysander. Use what you have learned from the activity on page 48 when you are thinking about Helena's reactions. But how should Lysander show the sudden transformation caused by the love-juice? Does he behave like the old Lysander, but simply directing his love towards someone else? Or does he now behave very differently (perhaps showing great physical passion for Helena), to show that he is under a magic spell?

Character review: Hermia (2)

'... what a dream was here!'
Draw a series of pictures to represent the dream that Hermia was having. What is the meaning of her dream, do you think?

138–139 **Or as ... deceive** and just as religious falsehoods (**heresies**) are hated most by the very men who were deceived by them

140 **surfeit ... heresy** excess ... false religious belief

141 **Of** by

142 **address** apply

146 **Ay me, for pity** *an expression of distress (like* **Alack**, *line 152)*

148 **Methought** it seemed to me

150 **removed** gone away

153 **swoon** faint

154 **nigh** near

Or as the heresies that men do leave,
Are hated most of those they did deceive;
So thou, my surfeit, and my heresy,   140
Of all be hated, but the most of me.
And, all my powers, address your love and might
To honour Helen, and to be her knight!

Exit.

HERMIA   (*awaking*)
Help me, Lysander, help me! do thy best
To pluck this crawling serpent from my breast!   145
Ay me, for pity! what a dream was here!
Lysander, look, how I do quake with fear.
Methought a serpent eat my heart away,
And you sat smiling at his cruel prey.
Lysander! what, removed? Lysander! lord!   150
What, out of hearing? Gone? No sound, no word?
Alack, where are you? Speak, and if you hear:
Speak, of all loves; I swoon almost with fear.
No? Then I will perceive you are not nigh.
Either death or you I'll find immediately.   155

Exit.

Exam practice

Themes: love (6)

'Love-in-idleness'

A Check pages 10 and 170 for background information on Cupid and then draw a cartoon strip to illustrate Oberon's story about Cupid and the flower (2.1.155–168).

B How would the magic flower be described if it were entered in a book of medicines? Fill in the following details, using Oberon's words (2.1.155–168) and the notes on page 36:

Name of flower:
   Alternative names:
Description:
Origin:
Powers:
Known antidotes:
Best method of applying it to the patient:

Now try selling the magic flower as a pharmaceutical product. Draw a design for the labels to go on the bottle (back and front), including the information that you have collected and any advertising slogans or special claims you think would help to sell it. You could find an interesting-looking bottle and stick the labels on.

C What view of love and its way of working is suggested by this story of Cupid, his arrow and the 'fair vestal' (2.1.155–164)? Retell it as a day-to-day story about the way love works on someone (or in this case, fails to work) without any divine intervention. What part has been played so far by accident and chance in the love affairs of the main characters?

Plot review (4): events in the wood

1. Draw a sketch-map of the wood and include the Duke's oak (1.2.105) and the bank where Titania sometimes lies (2.1.249–256). There will also be paths leading out of the wood to Athens in one direction and to Lysander's aunt's house in another. Work out the scale from 1.1.159 and 1.2.96. Then mark in pencil where you think the following characters are:
   • the four lovers (add the directions they are taking)
   • Titania (on her 'bank')
   • Puck and Oberon
   • the mechanicals (who have agreed to meet 'a mile without the town by moonlight' – 1.2.96–97).

2. The lovers are probably too busy rushing around and responding to changing circumstances, to sit down and write up their diaries. But imagine they take a few moments to scribble a few words on what has happened and how they feel. Write down each character's notes about events *as they see them* since their arrival in the wood.

Plot review (5): a strand chart

There are three strands to the plot of *A Midsummer Night's Dream*; they involve:
A the characters from the Athenian court
B the mechanicals
C the fairies.

Copy the following chart and add details to the relevant boxes, to show:
(a) what happens to the characters in that scene
(b) how their plot strand is linked to the other two strands in that scene.

To start you off, the boxes for Act 1 have been filled in. Complete the details for Act 2 and continue the chart after Acts 3, 4 and 5.

		Act 1, scene 1	Act 1, scene 2
Strand A The court and the lovers	Action	Theseus and Hippolyta prepare for for their wedding. Egeus forbids Hermia to marry Lysander. Hermia and Lysander plan to elope. Helena decides to tell Demetrius.	
	Links with Strand B	Philostrate goes off to organise wedding celebrations.	
	Links with Strand C	The lovers plan to run off to the wood.	
Strand B The mechanicals	Action		The mechanicals organise their play.
	Links with Strand A		The play is for the Duke's wedding.
	Links with Strand C		They plan to rehearse in the wood.
Strand C The fairies	Action		
	Links with Strand A		
	Links with Strand B		

Themes: love (7)

Women, men and power

A List the relationships in the play which show men exercising power over women.

B Imagine a discussion between Egeus and Hippolyta in which he argues why he is in the right to exercise such power over Hermia and she puts forward the opposite view. Write up the argument as a play script.

C Decide whether, in your opinion, the play (a) condemns this power-play, by attacking the ways in which the men exercise power over women; or (b) encourages us to feel that this is simply the way things are and that nothing can be done about it; or (c) goes as far as to support this state of affairs, suggesting that it is *right* for men to have power over women?

3.1 The wood

The mechanicals decide to hold their rehearsal in the clearing where, unknown to them, Titania is sleeping. Bottom is concerned that the death of Pyramus in the play will upset the ladies and Quince agrees to write an explanatory prologue.

Activities

Character review: Bottom (2)

His own prologue

Bottom has clearly been thinking about Quince's play since their first meeting. He is concerned that the women in the audience will be upset if they see him apparently killing himself and has worked out a solution: a prologue can explain that it's all make-believe.

Imagine that Bottom decides to try his hand at writing and drafts a prologue himself. Include the reassuring details that Bottom wants (lines 16–22) and write it 'in eight and eight' (see the note to line 24). Try to create the kind of poetry which would be typical of Bottom.

2   **Pat** promptly, on the dot

  convenient suitable

4   **brake** thicket, group of bushes

  tiring-house dressing-room

8   **bully** *a complimentary adjective, like 'good old Bottom'*

12   **abide** tolerate

13   **By'r lakin** *a mild oath:* By Our Lady (**lakin** = ladykin, little lady)

  parlous terrible (*from: perilous*)

16   **device** plan

17   **prologue** introductory speech (*as in Shakespeare's own* Henry V *or* Romeo and Juliet)

24   **in eight and six** *with alternate lines of eight and six syllables, the common metre for a ballad (or possibly, in the form of a sonnet, with eight lines – the octave – followed by six – the sestet)*

Act 3

Scene 1

The same place.

TITANIA *sleeps. Enter* QUINCE, SNUG, BOTTOM, FLUTE, SNOUT *and* STARVELING.

BOTTOM   Are we all met?

QUINCE   Pat, pat; and here's a marvellous convenient place
              for our rehearsal. This green plot shall be our
              stage, this hawthorn-brake our tiring-house; and
              we will do it in action, as we will do it before the   5
              Duke.

BOTTOM   Peter Quince?

QUINCE   What sayest thou, bully Bottom?

BOTTOM   There are things in this comedy of Pyramus and
              Thisby that will never please. First, Pyramus must   10
              draw a sword to kill himself; which the ladies
              cannot abide. How answer you that?

SNOUT   By 'r lakin, a parlous fear.

STARVELING   I believe we must leave the killing out, when all is
              done.   15

BOTTOM   Not a whit; I have a device to make all well. Write
              me a prologue, and let the prologue seem to say,
              we will do no harm with our swords, and that
              Pyramus is not killed indeed; and for the more
              better assurance, tell them that I Pyramus am not   20
              Pyramus, but Bottom the weaver; this will put
              them out of fear.

QUINCE   Well, we will have such a prologue; and it shall be
              written in eight and six.

BOTTOM   No, make it two more; let it be written in eight and   25
              eight.

SNOUT   Will not the ladies be afeard of the lion?

STARVELING   I fear it, I promise you.

3.1 The wood

They then decide that the actor playing the lion ought to explain that he is actually Snug the joiner (so as not to frighten people) and that one of them can represent the moon by entering with a thorn-bush and a lantern.

Activities

Shakespeare's language: malapropisms

The mechanicals speak in prose, but it is their own very colloquial version of English. They also have a habit of coming up with some amusing malapropisms. Find the following slips and complete a copy of the chart, explaining in each case (a) what the correct word was – the one that the character ought to have been using; (b) what meaning they were trying to get across; and (c) what the actual, mistaken, meaning was:

(a) Correct word	(b) Intended meaning	(c) Actual meaning

aggravate (1.2.76)
obscenely (1.2.103)
fowl (3.1.32)
defect (3.1.39)
disfigure (3.1.59)
odious (3.1.81)
Ninny (3.1.96)

How do each of the *actual* meanings add to the humour of the scene? For example, what picture do you conjure up of the mechanicals rehearsing *obscenely*; in what way might they *disfigure* moonshine; what is a *ninny*?

32 **fearful** (1) terrifying; (2) terrified (*as Snug might well be*)

39 **defect** Bottom means 'effect'

43 **pity of my life** the greatest pity

52 **almanac** calendar with astronomical data

55 **casement** part of a window opening on hinges

58–59 **bush ... lantern** The Man in the Moon was often represented carrying these objects.

59 **disfigure** he means 'figure' (represent)

BOTTOM	Masters, you ought to consider with yourself, to bring in, God shield us, a lion among ladies is a most dreadful thing: for there is not a more fearful wild fowl than your lion living; and we ought to look to 't.	30

SNOUT   Therefore another prologue must tell he is not a
          lion.   35

BOTTOM   Nay, you must name his name, and half his face
          must be seen through the lion's neck; and he
          himself must speak through, saying thus, or to
          the same defect: 'Ladies', or 'Fair ladies' 'I would
          wish you' or 'I would request you', or 'I would   40
          entreat you, not to fear, not to tremble: my life for
          yours. If you think I come hither as a lion, it were
          pity of my life. No, I am no such thing; I am a
          man as other men are'; and there indeed let him
          name his name, and tell them plainly he is Snug   45
          the joiner.

QUINCE   Well, it shall be so: but there is two hard things,
          that is, to bring the moonlight into a chamber;
          for, you know, Pyramus and Thisby meet by
          moonlight.   50

SNOUT   Doth the moon shine that night we play our play?

BOTTOM   A calender, a calender; look in the almanac; find
          out moonshine, find out moonshine.

QUINCE   Yes, it doth shine that night.

BOTTOM   Why, then may you leave a casement of the great   55
          chamber window, where we play, open, and the
          moon may shine in at the casement.

QUINCE   Ay, or else one must come in with a bush of thorns
          and a lantern, and say he comes to disfigure, or to
          present, the person of moonshine. Then there is   60
          another thing; we must have a wall in the great
          chamber; for Pyramus and Thisby, says the story,
          did talk through the chink of a wall.

SNOUT   You can never bring in a wall. What say you,

3.1 The wood

Bottom suggests that the wall which divides the lovers in the play can be represented by a man in an appropriate wall-like costume. As they begin their rehearsal, Puck enters to watch.

Activities

Themes: theatrical illusion (1)

Creating the play
Throughout *A Midsummer Night's Dream* we are being asked to think about dramatic illusion: the ways in which the theatre is capable of making us believe something, often by very simple means. An early example is Oberon's explanation 'I am invisible' (2.1.186). He simply tells us; and we accept that the lovers cannot see him (look back at the activity on page 38).

One of the charming things about the mechanicals is that they haven't much experience of the theatre and therefore are not aware of the conventions (customs and 'rules') that audiences are used to. Look back through this scene and 1.2.

1. What is it that the mechanicals fail to realise about theatre and illusion when they raise the 'problems' of:
   - the lion frightening the ladies (1.2.70–79 and 3.1.27–46)?
   - Pyramus killing himself (3.1.10–22)?
   - moonlight (3.1.47–60)?
   - the wall (3.1.60–70)?

continued on page 60

67–68 **loam ... rough-cast** clay ... lime and gravel plaster

74 **brake** thicket (*see line 4*)

76 **hempen home-spuns** shaggy yokels (*men wearing home-spun cloth made of hemp*)

78 **toward** in preparation

auditor member of the audience

81 **odious** hateful, repulsive

83 **odours savours sweet** fragrances smell sweetly

3.1

	Bottom?	65
BOTTOM	Some man or other must present Wall and let him have some plaster, or some loam, or some rough-cast about him, to signify wall; or let him hold his fingers thus; and through that cranny shall Pyramus and Thisby whisper.	70
QUINCE	If that may be, then all is well. Come, sit down, every mother's son, and rehearse your parts. Pyramus, you begin; when you have spoken your speech, enter into that brake; and so every one according to his cue.	75

Enter PUCK *behind.*

PUCK	What hempen home-spuns have we swaggering here, So near the cradle of the Fairy Queen? What, a play toward? I'll be an auditor; An actor too, perhaps, if I see cause.	
QUINCE	Speak, Pyramus. Thisby, stand forth.	80
BOTTOM *as* PYRAMUS	Thisby, the flowers of odious savours sweet.	
QUINCE	Odours, odours.	
BOTTOM *as* PYRAMUS	Odours savours sweet; So hath thy breath, my dearest Thisby dear. But hark, a voice! stay thou but here a while, And by and by I will to thee appear.	85

Exit behind.

PUCK	A stranger Pyramus than e'er played here!	
FLUTE	Must I speak now?	
QUINCE	Ay, marry, must you; for you must understand, he goes but to see a noise that he heard, and is to come again.	90
FLUTE *as* THISBE	Most radiant Pyramus, most lily-white of hue, Of colour like the red rose on triumphant brier,	

3.1 The wood

When Bottom goes 'off-stage' after delivering one of his speeches, Puck mischievously gives him an ass's head. When he returns, unaware of his new head, the others are horrified by the sight and run off in terror.

Activities

2. What is essentially 'untheatrical' about the solutions they come up with in each case? (Why are they wrong or unnecessary?)
3. Which two features of play-acting is Flute ignorant about? (Look at 3.1.88–100.)
4. Study the pictures of Shakespeare's playhouse on pages 167–168. Where do you think the actor playing Quince might have gestured, when he pointed out 'this green plot' and 'this hawthorn break' (lines 3–4)?
5. What would your solutions have been to the mechanicals' four 'problems', if you had been planning to perform 'Pyramus and Thisby' on Shakespeare's stage?

94 **brisky juvenal** lively youth
   eke also

98–99 **all your part at once** *Each actor would only be given his 'part' of the play: his own lines, plus the other characters' cue lines.*

108 **fire** *Puck was associated with Will-o'-the-Wisp (the ghostly flame caused by marsh-gas).*

111 **knavery** dirty trick

John Carlisle as Oberon (RSC 1989)

	Most brisky juvenal, and eke most lovely Jew,	
	As truest horse, that yet would never tire.	95
	I'll meet thee, Pyramus, at Ninny's tomb.	

QUINCE   Ninus' tomb, man! Why, you must not speak that
          yet; that you answer to Pyramus: you speak all
          your part at once, cues and all. Pyramus, enter:
          your cue is past; it is 'never tire'.   100

FLUTE *as*   O, – As true as truest horse, that yet would never tire.
THISBE

Re-enter BOTTOM *wearing an ass's head.*

BOTTOM *as*   If I were fair, Thisby, I were only thine.
PYRAMUS

QUINCE   O monstrous! O strange! We are haunted; pray,
          masters, fly! masters, help!

Exeunt all but BOTTOM *and* PUCK.

PUCK   (*coming forward*)
          I'll follow you, I'll lead you about a round,   105
          Through bog, through bush, through brake,
            through brier;
          Sometime a horse I'll be, sometime a hound,
          A hog, a headless bear, sometime a fire;
          And neigh, and bark, and grunt, and roar, and
            burn,
          Like horse, hound, hog, bear, fire, at every turn. 110

Exit.

BOTTOM   Why do they run away? This is a knavery of them
          to make me afeard.

Re-enter SNOUT.

SNOUT   O Bottom, thou art changed! What do I see on
          thee?

BOTTOM   What do you see? You see an ass-head of your   115
          own, do you?

Exit SNOUT.

3.1 The wood

Left alone, Bottom decides that the others are playing a game and are trying to frighten him. As he sings to keep his spirits up, Titania awakes at the sound and declares her love for him.

Activities

Actors' interpretations: Key moments

Look back at the following key moments and think about the different ways in which they might be performed:

- lines 68–69: How does Wall hold his fingers to represent the chink? Try some different movements and gestures to gain a comic effect.
- lines 101–103: Freeze-frame the moment when Bottom re-enters transformed.
- line 127: Where has Titania been sleeping? In several productions recently, she has been asleep in a bed, which has been hoisted up above the stage and lowered when Bottom starts singing. What are the advantages and disadvantages of arranging it in this way?
- line 131: Does Bottom give a donkey's bray on 'nay'?
- What should he look like? Study the photographs on pages 68 and 104 and devise your own version. Is it better for him to wear a complete ass's head, or for his own face to be seen? Does he move differently? (Daniel Ryan in 1999 started to plod like a donkey.)

117 **translated** turned by magic into something else

123 **ousel** blackbird

125 **throstle** thrush

126 **quill** shrill song

129 **plain-song** with its simple melody

132 **set his wit** *Bottom is thinking about the proverb which says that it's a waste of time using your intelligence to answer a fool.*

133 **give ... the lie** tell the bird it was a liar

134 **cry 'cuckoo'** *perhaps:* call you a cuckold (*a man whose wife has been unfaithful*)

136 **is much enamoured of** has fallen in love with

137 **enthrallèd to thy shape** captivated by your physical appearance

138 **And thy ... move me** and the power of your beautiful qualities forces me

144 **gleek** make a satirical joke

Re-enter QUINCE.

QUINCE   Bless thee Bottom, bless thee! thou art translated!

Exit.

BOTTOM   I see their knavery: this is to make an ass of me, to
fright me, if they could; but I will not stir from
this place, do what they can. I will walk up and   120
down here, and I will sing, that they shall hear I
am not afraid. (*Sings.*)
    The ousel cock, so black of hue,
    With orange-tawny bill,
    The throstle with his note so true,   125
    The wren with little quill.

TITANIA   (*awaking*)
What angel wakes me from my flowery bed?

BOTTOM   (*sings*)
    The finch, the sparrow, and the lark,
    The plain-song cuckoo grey;
    Whose note full many a man doth mark,   130
    And dares not answer 'nay'.
For indeed, who would set his wit to so foolish a
bird? Who would give a bird the lie, though he
cry 'cuckoo' never so?

TITANIA   I pray thee, gentle mortal, sing again;   135
Mine ear is much enamoured of thy note;
So is mine eye enthrallèd to thy shape;
And thy fair virtue's force perforce doth move me
On the first view, to say, to swear I love thee.

BOTTOM   Methinks, mistress, you should have little reason   140
for that: and yet, to say the truth, reason and love
keep little company together nowadays. The more
the pity that some honest neighbours will not
make them friends. Nay, I can gleek upon
occasion.   145

TITANIA   Thou art as wise as thou art beautiful.

BOTTOM   Not so, neither; but if I had wit enough to get out
of this wood, I have enough to serve mine own

3.1 The wood

Titania refuses to let Bottom leave the wood and summons her fairies (Peaseblossom, Cobweb, Moth and Mustardseed) to tend upon him.

Activities

Themes: love (8)

Reason and love
Bottom says that 'reason and love keep little company together nowadays' (lines 141–142). What evidence can you find in the play so far to show that people in love do not use their powers of reasoning? Does the magic love-juice cause people to lose their reason?

Character review: Bottom (3)

His thoughts and feelings
Write notes to describe Bottom's changing thoughts, from the point where he returns to the rehearsal (line 101) to the appearance of the four fairies (line 160). Make sure that the thoughts fit the character that he has displayed so far, and try to write as he would speak.

151 **whether ... or no** whether you want to or not

152 **rate** rank, value

153 **The summer ... state** summer always (**still**) follows wherever I go

158 **purge thy mortal grossness** purify you of your human physical form

164 **dewberries** blackberries (*or possibly:* gooseberries)

167 **And for night-tapers ... thighs** collect wax from the bees' thighs to make night-lights

turn.

TITANIA	Out of this wood do not desire to go; 150
	Thou shalt remain here, whether thou wilt or no.
	I am a spirit of no common rate;
	The summer still doth tend upon my state,
	And I do love thee; therefore, go with me.
	I'll give thee fairies to attend on thee; 155
	And they shall fetch thee jewels from the deep,
	And sing, while thou on pressèd flowers dost sleep:
	And I will purge thy mortal grossness so
	That thou shalt like an airy spirit go.
	Peaseblossom, Cobweb, Moth, and Mustardseed! 160

Enter Four Fairies.

FIRST FAIRY   Ready

SECOND   And I.
  FAIRY

THIRD FAIRY   And I.

FOURTH FAIRY   And I.

ALL   Where shall we go?

TITANIA	Be kind and courteous to this gentleman;
	Hop in his walks, and gambol in his eyes;
	Feed him with apricocks and dewberries,
	With purple grapes, green figs, and mulberries; 165
	The honey-bags steal from the humble-bees,
	And for night-tapers crop their waxen thighs,
	And light them at the fiery glow-worm's eyes,
	To have my love to bed, and to arise;
	And pluck the wings from painted butterflies 170
	To fan the moonbeams from his sleeping eyes;
	Nod to him, elves, and do him courtesies.

FIRST FAIRY   Hail, mortal!

3.1 The wood

Bottom introduces himself to each of the fairies and Titania orders them to lead him to her bower.

Activities

Actors' interpretations: Bottom's humour

Act out the scene from the departure of Quince (line 104) to the end, bringing out as much of the humour as you can.

- Work out a tune to fit Bottom's song (lines 123–131). Does he sing badly or well?
- How does he react when he first hears Titania's voice?
- How does he respond to Titania's first declaration of love (lines 135–139) and her compliment (line 146)?
- Does Titania accompany her offers (lines 155–159) with any particular actions?
- Notice that Bottom addresses the four new fairies as 'Master' (lines 178–191). Having the fairies played by girls is a recent tradition. Should they be played by males or females, young or old, in your opinion?
- How can you bring out the meanings of Bottom's special jokes with each fairy (lines 177–190)?
- Some people see a bawdy double meaning in 'to arise' (line 169). How sexual and physical should Titania's behaviour be?
- Does Bottom make a noise or do something to prompt Titania's last line (line 196)?

174 **I cry ... mercy** I beg your pardon

beseech beg

178 **cut my finger** *Cobwebs were wrapped around cuts to stop bleeding.*

179 **honest gentleman** my good sir

181 **Squash** unripe pea-pod (**Peascod**, *line 182*)

186 **your patience** what you put up with

188 **house** family (*the same as* **kindred**, *line 189*)

193–194 **The moon ... flower** *Some people believed that dew came from the moon.*

195 **Lamenting ... chastity** *The moon goddess, Diana, was also the goddess of chastity and would weep over any violated virgin. (See page 170.)*

3.1

SECOND FAIRY	Hail!
THIRD FAIRY	Hail!
FOURTH FAIRY	Hail!
BOTTOM	I cry your worships mercy heartily; I beseech your worship's name? 175
FIRST FAIRY	Cobweb.
BOTTOM	I shall desire you of more acquaintance, good Master Cobweb: if I cut my finger, I shall make bold with you. Your name, honest gentleman?
SECOND FAIRY	Peaseblossom. 180
BOTTOM	I pray you, commend me to Mistress Squash, your mother, and to Master Peascod, your father. Good Master Peaseblossom, I shall desire you of more acquaintance too. Your name, I beseech you, sir?
THIRD FAIRY	Mustardseed. 185
BOTTOM	Good Master Mustardseed, I know your patience well: that same cowardly, giant-like ox-beef hath devoured many a gentleman of your house. I promise you, your kindred hath made my eyes water ere now. I desire you of more acquaintance, 190 good Master Mustardseed.
TITANIA	Come, wait upon him, lead him to my bower. The moon, methinks, looks with a watery eye, And when she weeps, weeps every little flower, Lamenting some enforcéd chastity. 195 Tie up my love's tongue, bring him silently.

Exeunt behind.

3.2 The wood

Puck reports to Oberon what happened with the mechanicals and how Titania has fallen in love with an ass.

Activities

Plot review (6): Puck's mischief

Puck's account of his trick on Bottom adds some details to the scene which we might not otherwise know. Imagine you were filming the play and wanted to illustrate Puck's words with a flashback. Draw a sequence of storyboard frames to show what the flashback would look like.

Stella Gonet as Titania and Des Barrit as Bottom (RSC 1994)

---

3 **in extremity** desperately

5 **night-rule** night-time activity

7 **close and consecrated** secret and holy

8 **dull** drowsy

9 **patches, rude mechanicals** clowns, rough workmen

12 **nuptial-day** wedding day

13 **shallowest … sort** the dimmest idiot in that stupid gang

15 **forsook his scene** left the stage

17 **nole** head (noddle)

18 **Anon** straightaway

19 **mimic** actor

20 **As wild … eye** just like wild geese who spot a hunter creeping up on them

21 **russet-pated choughs** grey-headed jackdaws

 sort flock

23 **sever** divide

25 **stamp** *Some editions change this to 'stump'.*

26 **He** another of them

27–28 *Because they had lost their senses and were frightened, they began to think that lifeless objects were attacking them.*

30 **from yielders … catch** (*a proverb:*) everybody will steal from cowards

32 **translated** transformed

Scene 2

Another part of the wood.

Enter OBERON.

OBERON   I wonder if Titania be awaked;
Then, what it was that next came in her eye,
Which she must dote on in extremity.

Enter PUCK.

Here comes my messenger. How now, mad spirit!
What night-rule now about this haunted grove?   5

PUCK   My mistress with a monster is in love.
Near to her close and consecrated bower,
While she was in her dull and sleeping hour,
A crew of patches, rude mechanicals,
That work for bread upon Athenian stalls,   10
Were met together to rehearse a play
Intended for great Theseus' nuptial-day.
The shallowest thick-skin of that barren sort,
Who Pyramus presented, in their sport
Forsook his scene and entered in a brake;   15
When I did him at this advantage take,
An ass's nole I fixéd on his head.
Anon his Thisbe must be answeréd,
And forth my mimic comes. When they him spy,
As wild geese that the creeping fowler eye,   20
Or russet-pated choughs, many in sort,
Rising and cawing at the gun's report,
Sever themselves and madly sweep the sky,
So at his sight, away his fellows fly;
And at our stamp here, o'er and o'er one falls;   25
He 'murder' cries, and help from Athens calls.
Their sense thus weak, lost with their fears thus
    strong,
Made senseless things begin to do them wrong;
For briers and thorns at their apparel snatch;
Some sleeves, some hats; from yielders all things
    catch.   30
I led them on in this distracted fear,
And left sweet Pyramus translated there;

3.2 The wood

When Hermia enters, pursued by Demetrius, Puck admits that, although this is the woman he saw earlier, this is not the man he anointed with the juice. They watch as Hermia accuses Demetrius of having murdered Lysander in his sleep.

Activities

Actors' interpretations: 'This is the woman, but not this the man.'

How does Puck say the second half of this line (line 42)? As though he is, for example:

- amused?
- frightened that Oberon will punish his mistake?
- puzzled?

The way he says it will depend upon (a) his relationship with Oberon; and (b) his attitude towards his pranks (see the activity on page 72).

Themes: order and disorder (2)

'This whole earth ...'
Draw a picture to illustrate Hermia's image of the sun boring a hole through the earth (lines 52–55). What is the connection between that image and the vision of disorder conjured up by Titania's speech earlier (2.1.88–114)?

36 **latched** moistened

40 **That ... eyed** So that, when he wakes, he cannot avoid seeing her

41 **Stand close** keep out of sight

44 **Lay ... foe** save such bitter words for your worst enemy

45 **Now ... chide** at the moment I'm only scolding

use treat

48 **o'er shoes in** ankle-deep in

53 **whole** solid

53–55 **This whole ... Antipodes** *She imagines the moon boring through the centre of the earth and disturbing the sun's (***Her brother's***) noon on the other side of the world (***the Antipodes***) by bringing darkness.*

57 **dead** deadly

61 **yonder Venus** the planet Venus up there in its shining orbit (**sphere**, *see 2.1.7*)

When in that moment, so it came to pass,
Titania waked, and straightway loved an ass.

OBERON   This falls out better than I could devise.   35
But hast thou yet latched the Athenian's eyes
With the love-juice, as I did bid thee do?

PUCK   I took him sleeping – that is finished too –
And the Athenian woman by his side;
That, when he waked, of force she must be eyed.   40

Enter DEMETRIUS *and* HERMIA.

OBERON   Stand close: this is the same Athenian.

PUCK   This is the woman, but not this the man.

DEMETRIUS   O, why rebuke you him that loves you so?
Lay breath so bitter on your bitter foe.

HERMIA   Now I but chide, but I should use thee worse,   45
For thou, I fear, hast given me cause to curse.
If thou hast slain Lysander in his sleep,
Being o'er shoes in blood, plunge in the deep,
And kill me too.
The sun was not so true unto the day   50
As he to me. Would he have stolen away
From sleeping Hermia? I'll believe as soon
This whole earth may be bored, and that the moon
May through the centre creep, and so displease
Her brother's noontide with the Antipodes.   55
It cannot be but thou hast murdered him;
So should a murderer look; so dead, so grim.

DEMETRIUS   So should the murdered look; and so should I,
Pierced through the heart with your stern cruelty:
Yet you, the murderer, look as bright, as clear   60
As yonder Venus in her glimmering sphere.

HERMIA   What's this to my Lysander? Where is he?
Ah, good Demetrius, wilt thou give him me?

DEMETRIUS   I had rather give his carcass to my hounds.

3.2 The wood

Hermia runs off angrily and the exhausted Demetrius lies down and sleeps. Rebuking Puck for his mistake, Oberon orders him to search through the wood and find Helena.

Activities

Actors' interpretations: sleepiness

In many productions the sleepiness which comes over Demetrius (lines 82–87) – and other characters later – is actually induced by a magic spell from Oberon. What might Oberon do? In pairs work out some convincing action which would indicate to the audience that Oberon is magicking Demetrius asleep.

Character review: Oberon (2)

His relationship with Puck
What kind of relationship do Oberon and Puck have? Are there moments when you have seen the following kinds of relationship? If so, when?

- King and important subject
- King and lowly subject
- Master and servant
- Father and son
- Brothers
- Friends
- Professional colleagues

Any other kind?

67 **Henceforth ... men!** you're not a human being any longer!

69 **Durst** did you dare

70 **O brave touch!** *(ironic)*

71 **worm** serpent

72–73 **for with ... stung** no adder ever stung with as double (= (1) forked; (2) deceitful) a tongue

74 **You spend ... mood** the anger you're giving vent to is based on a misunderstanding

76 **aught** anything

78 **An if ... therefore** even if I could, what would I get for it?

82 **vein** mood

84–85 **For sorrow's ... owe** misery makes you drowsy, especially because it has already led to sleeplessness

86–87 **Which now ... stay** *Demetrius continues the money image: sleep will pay some of the money it owes, if he stays here and accepts its offer (*tender*).*

90 **Of thy misprision ... ensue** Your mistake must inevitably lead to

92–93 **Then fate ... oath** If that's the case, fate has taken charge; since, for every man who remains faithful, there are a million who don't, and break one oath after another

95 **look** make sure

96 **fancy-sick ... cheer** love-sick and pale in the face

| HERMIA | Out, dog! out, cur! thou drivest me past the | |
| | bounds | 65 |

HERMIA   Out, dog! out, cur! thou drivest me past the
        bounds   65
    Of maiden's patience. Hast thou slain him, then?
    Henceforth be never numbered among men!
    O, once tell true; tell true, even for my sake:
    Durst thou have looked upon him, being awake?
    And hast thou killed him sleeping? O brave touch!   70
    Could not a worm, an adder do so much?
    An adder did it: for with doubler tongue
    Than thine, thou serpent, never adder stung.

DEMETRIUS   You spend your passion on a misprised mood:
    I am not guilty of Lysander's blood;   75
    Nor is he dead, for aught that I can tell.

HERMIA   I pray thee tell me then that he is well.

DEMETRIUS   An if I could, what should I get therefore?

HERMIA   A privilege never to see me more.
    And from thy hated presence part I so: 80
    See me no more, whether he be dead or no.

Exit.

DEMETRIUS   There is no following her in this fierce vein;
    Here therefore for a while I will remain.
    So sorrow's heaviness doth heavier grow
    For debt that bankrupt sleep doth sorrow owe,   85
    Which now in some slight measure it will pay,
    It for his tender here I make some stay.

Lies down and sleeps.

OBERON   What hast thou done? Thou hast mistaken quite,
    And laid the love-joice on some true-love's sight.
    Of thy misprision must perforce ensue   90
    Some true love turned, and not a false turned true.

PUCK   Then fate o'er-rules, that, one man holding troth,
    A million fail, confounding oath on oath.

OBERON   About the wood go swifter than the wind,
    And Helena of Athens look thou find.   95
    All fancy-sick she is and pale of cheer

3.2 The wood

As Oberon is putting the juice on Demetrius's eyes, so that he will fall in love with Helena when he wakes up, she arrives on the scene, pursued by Lysander (now under the influence of the juice himself and in love with her).

Activities

Character review: Puck (3)

His part in the action
Look back at the following actions by Puck:

- collecting the love-in-idleness for Oberon (2.1)
- putting an ass's head on Bottom and then terrifying the other mechanicals (3.1)
- observing what happened when Titania awoke and recounting it to Oberon (3.2.6–34)
- realising what might happen, now that he has anointed Lysander's eyes in mistake for Demetrius's (3.2.92–121).

Imagine Puck had been invited to give an after-dinner speech to the Ancient Order of Hobgoblins. Write his speech, in which he refers to these events and makes it clear how he feels about his involvement in them. (Which of these actions do you think will have given him particular delight?) Then perform the speech in the character of Puck.

97 **the fresh blood** *People believed that a drop of blood was lost every time you sighed.*

98 **illusion** trick, deception

99 **against** ready for when

101 **Tartar's bow** *The Tartars from central Asia were famous bowmen.*

103 **Cupid's archery** *see 2.1.155–168*

104 **apple** pupil

113 **fee** reward

114 **fond** foolish

122 **in scorn** in mockery

124 **Look when** whenever

124–125 **and vows ... appears** when oaths are 'born' in tears, they must be true

With sight of love that cost the fresh blood dear.
By some illusion see thou bring her here;
I'll charm his eyes against she do appear.

PUCK   I go, I go, look how I go,   100
                Swifter than arrow from the Tartar's bow.

                                                                    Exit.

OBERON   Flower of this purple dye,
                Hit with Cupid's archery,
                Sink in apple of his eye.
                When his love he doth espy,   105
                Let her shine as gloriously
                As the Venus of the sky.
                When thou wak'st, if she be by,
                Beg of her for remedy.

Re-enter PUCK. *Squeezes the juice on* DEMETRIUS's *eyes.*

PUCK   Captain of our fairy band,   110
                Helena is here at hand,
                And the youth, mistook by me,
                Pleading for a lover's fee.
                Shall we their fond pageant see?
                Lord, what fools these mortals be!   115

OBERON   Stand aside: the noise they make
                Will cause Demetrius to awake.

PUCK   Then will two at once woo one;
                That must needs be sport alone;
                And those things do best please me   120
                That befall preposterously.

They stand behind.

Enter LYSANDER *and* HELENA.

LYSANDER   Why should you think that I should woo in scorn?
                Scorn and derision never come in tears:
                Look when I vow I weep; and vows so born
                In their nativity all truth appears.   125
                How can these things in me seem scorn to you,
                Bearing the badge of faith to prove them true?

3.2 The wood

As Lysander unsuccessfully woos Helena, Demetrius wakes up and declares his love for her. She now believes that both the men are making fun of her.

Activities

Character review: the lovers (1)

'O Helen, goddess …'

1. In groups of five (Oberon, Puck and the three lovers), freeze-frame the moment when Demetrius awakes (line 137). Then get each person to say what their character is thinking and feeling in that instant.
2. Hot-seat Helena to find out what she thinks is going on and how she hopes it will be sorted out.

Plot review (7): the lovers

Who loves whom?

Look back at the activity on page 46 and draw a Phase 3 version of your lovers' diagram, showing who now loves whom (from 3.2.137). Colour-code any characters who are under the spell of the magic love-juice.

129 **When troth … fray** the promise (**truth** 1) you give to me destroys your faithfulness (**truth** 2) to Hermia; a fight for good and bad!

131 **nothing weigh** be able to weigh nothing (*because the scales will be balanced – see lines 132–133*)

133 **light as tales** light = (1) lightweight; (2) false; tales = (1) empty talk; (2) lies

138 **eyne** eyes

141 **congealéd** frozen

Taurus *a mountain range in Turkey*

144 **seal** pledge, promise

145 **bent** determined

147 **civil** polite

knew courtesy were acquainted with good manners

148 **do me … injury** insult me so much

150 **join in souls** combine with the same aim

152 **use** treat

153 **superpraise my parts** overdo your praise of my qualities

157 **trim** fine (*she is being ironic*)

158 **conjure** raise (*like a spirit*)

159 **sort** rank

160 **extort** take away

161 **make you sport** give you some fun

HELENA	You do advance your cunning more and more.
	When truth kills truth, O devilish-holy fray!
	These vows are Hermia's: will you give her o'er? 130
	Weigh oath with oath, and you will nothing weigh.
	Your vows to her and me, put in two scales,
	Will even weigh; and both as light as tales.
LYSANDER	I had no judgement when to her I swore.
HELENA	Nor none, in my mind, now you give her o'er. 135
LYSANDER	Demetrius loves her, and he loves not you.
DEMETRIUS	(awaking)
	O Helen, goddess, nymph, perfect, divine,
	To what, my love, shall I compare thine eyne?
	Crystal is muddy: O how ripe in show
	Thy lips, those kissing cherries, tempting grow! 140
	That pure congealéd white, high Taurus' snow,
	Fanned with the eastern wind, turns to a crow
	When thou hold'st up thy hand. O let me liss
	This princess of pure white, this seal of bliss!
HELENA	O spite! O hell! I see you all are bent 145
	To set against me for your merriment:
	If you were civil, and knew courtesy,
	You would not do me thus much injury.
	Can you not hate me, as I know you do,
	But you must join in souls to mock me too? 150
	If you were men, as men you are in show,
	You would not use a gentle lady so;
	To vow, and swear, and superpraise my parts,
	When I am sure you hate me with your hearts.
	You both are rivals, and love Hermia; 155
	And now both rivals, to mock Helena.
	A trim exploit, a manly enterprise,
	To conjure tears up in a poor maid's eyes
	With your derision! None of noble sort
	Would so offend a virgin, and extort 160
	A poor soul's patience, all to make you sport.
LYSANDER	You are unkind, Demetrius; be not so;
	For you love Hermia; this you know I know;
	And here with all good will, with all my heart,

3.2 The wood

When Hermia arrives on the scene, she cannot understand why Lysander had left her alone and she is shocked when he tells her he hates her. Helena now decides that Hermia must be in on the men's plot to make fun of her.

Activities

Character review: the lovers (2)

Under a spell

It's worth recalling at this point that the men are under a spell, but the women aren't: it is little wonder that Helena and Hermia haven't got a clue what the men are up to. If you were directing the play, would you want to show that the men were under a spell? What would be the advantages and disadvantages? How might you show it?

Actors' interpretations: observing the lovers

What should Puck and Oberon do throughout this long scene? Hide themselves away, so that the audience stop noticing them? Move invisibly around the lovers? Talk about the advantages and disadvantages of the different possibilities.

166 **bequeath** hand over

169 **I will none** I want nothing to do with her

171 **but as ... sojourned** was staying with her temporarily, like a guest

174 **Disparage ... know** don't criticise the love you're not experiencing yourself

175 **aby it dear** pay dearly for it

177–180 **Dark night ... recompense** the darkness has taken away the power of sight but has sharpened the sense of hearing; it obstructs sight but doubly improves hearing

186 **bide** stay

187 **engilds** turns to gold

188 **oes** silver spangles (**oes and eyes**: stars)

192 **confederacy** group of plotters

194 **in spite of me** to spite me

In Hermia's love I yield you up my part;   165
And yours of Helena to me bequeath,
Whom I do love, and will do till my death.

HELENA   Never did mockers waste more idle breath.

DEMETRIUS   Lysander, keep thy Hermia; I will none.
If e'er I loved her, all that love is gone.   170
My heart to her but as guest-wise sojourned,
And now to Helen is it home returned,
There to remain.

LYSANDER   Helen, it is not so.

DEMETRIUS   Disparage not the faith thou dost not know,
Lest to thy peril thou aby it dear.   175
Look where thy love comes; yonder is thy dear.

     Enter HERMIA.

HERMIA   Dark night, that from the eye his function takes,
The ear more quick of apprehension makes;
Wherein it doth impair the seeing sense,
It pays the hearing double recompense.   180
Thou art not by mine eye, Lysander, found;
Mine ear, I thank it, brought me to thy sound.
But why unkindly didst thou leave me so?

LYSANDER   Why should he stay whom love doth press to go?

HERMIA   What love could press Lysander from my side?   185

LYSANDER   Lysander's love, that would not let him bide;
Fair Helena, who more engilds the night
Than all you fiery oes and eyes of light.
Why seek'st thou me? Could not this make thee know
The hate I bare thee made me leave thee so?   190

HERMIA   You speak not as you think; it cannot be.

HELENA   Lo, she is one of this confederacy!
Now I perceive they have conjoined, all three,
To fashion this false sport in spite of me.
Injurious Hermia, most ungrateful maid!   195
Have you conspired, have you with these contrived

3.2 The wood

Helena reminds Hermia that they used to be such close friends and tells her how upset she is that Hermia has joined in with the men's game of teasing her.

Activities

Character review: Helena (4)

'Lo, she is one ...!'
How should Helena deliver her long speech (line 192)? She seems to move from one tone to another. Practise the speech, first trying the following tones on the lines indicated:

- as though making an amazing – and not pleasant – discovery (lines 192–194)
- angrily (lines 195–197)
- disappointedly (lines 198–202)
- nostalgically and sentimentally (lines 203–214)
- threateningly (lines 215–219).

Try other ways in which she might deliver the speech. Which works best, in your opinion, bearing in mind what you have seen of Helena so far?

197 **bait** torment

198 **counsel** secrets

200 **chid** complained at

203 **artificial gods** *people who could create things (like gods) skilfully (with artifice)*

205 **sampler** *piece of embroidery*

208 **incorporate** in one body

210 **an union in partition** united, even though two individuals

213 **two of the first ...** two bodies

coats coats of arms, crowned with a single crest (*line 214*), belonging to one person

215 **rent ... asunder** tear apart

218 **Our sex** women generally

225 **even but now** only recently

227 **celestial** heavenly

230 **tender** offer

231 **But by** unless it's by

232 **in grace** blessed

To bait me with this foul derision?
Is all the counsel that we two have shared,
The sisters' vows, the hours that we have spent,
When we have chid the hasty-footed time   200
For parting us, – O, is all forgot?
All school-days' friendship, childhood innocence?
We, Hermia, like two artificial gods,
Have with our needles created both one flower,
Both on one sampler, sitting on one cushion,   205
Both warbling of one song, both in one key;
As if our hands, our sides, voices, and minds
Had been incorporate. So we grew together,
Like to a double cherry, seeming parted,
But yet an union in partition,   210
Two lovely berries, moulded on one stem;
So, with two seeming bodies, but one heart;
Two of the first, like coats in heraldry,
Due but to one and crownéd with one crest.
And will you rent our ancient love asunder,   215
To join with men in scorning your poor friend?
It is not friendly, 't is not maidenly.
Our sex, as well as I, may chide you for it,
Though I alone do feel the injury.

HERMIA   I am amazéd at your passionate words;   220
I scorn you not; it seems that you scorn me.

HELENA   Have you not set Lysander, as in scorn,
To follow me, and praise my eyes and face?
And made your other love, Demetrius,
Who even but now did spurn me with his foot,   225
To call me goddess, nymph, divine, and rare,
Precious, celestial? Wherefore speaks he this
To her he hates? And wherefore doth Lysander
Deny your love, so rich within his soul,
And tender me, forsooth! affection,   230
But by your setting on, by your consent?
What though I be not so in grace as you,
So hung upon with love, so fortunate?
But miserable most, to love unloved.
This you should pity rather than despise.   235

HERMIA   I understand not what you mean by this.

3.2 The wood

Convinced that the other three are in league to make fun of her, Helena tries to leave, but is stopped by Demetrius and Lysander, who keep declaring their love.

Activities

Actors' interpretations: stage activity

In most productions there is some very physical stage business at this point. Use the stage plan on page 168 to 'block' lines 237–263 (mark in the actors' movements). Draw as many diagrams as you need and add annotations to explain what the actors are doing at different times. Rough sketches of particular moments in the scene will help too. Look especially at:

- Lysander calling Helena back (line 245 – does he go to her?)
- Demetrius and Lysander beginning to argue (lines 248–255 – what do they do?)
- Hermia holding on to Lysander (line 260 – but where does she start to do this, and what exactly does she do?).

Demetrius (Paul Lacoux), Hermia (Amanda Bellamy) and Lysander (Stephen Simms) in the 1989 RSC production

237 **Ay, do, persever** OK, go on, keep it up

counterfeit put on

238 **make mouths** make faces

240 **chronicled** put on record

247 **O, excellent!** (*ironic*)

248 **If she … compel** if her requests don't work, I can use force

252 **that which I will lose** his life (*if he fights a duel for her*)

255 **withdraw** come away (*to fight*)

256 **whereto tends all this?** What's this all about?

257 **Ethiope** *a term for anyone with a black skin; Demetrius is insulting Hermia for her dark complexion, which was unfashionable in the days of fair-haired Queen Elizabeth.*

258–259 **Seem to … not** he's pretending he's trying to pull away from her, in order to follow me, but he doesn't get anywhere

259 **tame** cowardly, easily controlled

260 **burr** *prickly seed-case which sticks to clothes*

262 **rude** rough

3.2

HELENA	Ay, do, perséver, counterfeit sad looks,
	Make mouths upon me when I turn my back,
	Wink each at other, hold the sweet jest up:
	This sport, well carried, shall be chronicled. 240
	If you have any pity, grace, or manners,
	You would not make me such an argument.
	But fare ye well; 't is partly mine own fault,
	Which death or absence soon shall remedy.
LYSANDER	Stay, gentle Helena, hear my excuse; 245
	My love, my life, my soul, fair Helena!
HELENA	O, excellent!
HERMIA	Sweet, do not scorn her so.
DEMETRIUS	If she cannot entreat, I can compel.
LYSANDER	Thou canst compel no more than she entreat.
	Thy threats have no more strength than her weak
	prayers. 250
	Helen, I love thee, by my life I do;
	I swear by that which I will lose for thee
	To prove him false that says I love thee not.
DEMETRIUS	I say I love thee more than he can do.
LYSANDER	If thou say so, withdraw and prove it too. 255
DEMETRIUS	Quick, come.
HERMIA	Lysander, whereto tends all this?
LYSANDER	Away, you Ethiope.
DEMETRIUS	No, no, sir,
	Seem to break loose; take on as you would follow,
	But yet come not; you are a tame man, go!
LYSANDER	(*struggling with* HERMIA)
	Hang off, thou cat, thou burr; vile thing, let loose, 260
	Or I will shake thee from me like a serpent!
HERMIA	Why are you grown so rude? What change is this,
	Sweet love?

3.2 The wood

Hermia tries to hang on to Lysander, but he throws her off. Now convinced that Lysander really has rejected her, Hermia turns on Helena, accusing her of stealing Lysander's affections, and the two women begin to argue.

Activities

Actors' interpretations: which is which?

This photograph shows Hermia and Helena in the RSC 1994 production. How can you tell which is which?

Which part of the scene does this photograph come from?

What else does the photograph tell you about the style of the production?

Emma Fielding as Hermia and Haydn Gwynne as Helena (RSC 1994)

263 **tawny** swarthy (*see line 257*)

264 **medicine ... potion** *both could mean poison*

267 **bond** (1) tie; (2) promise

274 **erewhile** a little while ago

282 **juggler** trickster

canker-blossom maggot (*which eats away at the 'blossom' of love*)

284 **Fine, I' faith** O, very nice! (*ironic*)

288 **counterfeit** fake

puppet (1) dwarf; (2) *Helena thinks Hermia is simply playing a part*

291 **urged** brought into the argument

292 **personage** dignified person

293 **prevailed with him** won him over

LYSANDER	Thy love? out, tawny Tartar, out! Out, loathéd medicine; hated potion, hence!
HERMIA	Do you not jest?
HELENA	Yes, sooth, and so do you.

265

LYSANDER	Demetrius, I will keep my word with thee.
DEMETRIUS	I would I had your bond; for I perceive A weak bond holds you; I'll not trust your word.
LYSANDER	What, should I hurt her, strike her, kill her dead? Although I hate her, I'll not harm her so.

270

HERMIA	What, can you do me greater harm than hate? Hate me? Wherefore? O me, what news, my love! Am not I Hermia? Are not you Lysander? I am as fair now as I was erewhile. Since night you loved me; yet since night you left me. Why then, you left me – O, the gods forbid! – In earnest, shall I say?

275

LYSANDER	Ay, by my life: And never did desire to see thee more. Therefore be out of hope, of question, of doubt; Be certain, nothing truer, 't is no jest That I do hate thee, and love Helena.

280

HERMIA	O me! you juggler, you canker-blossom, You thief of love! What, have you come by night And stolen my love's heart from him?
HELENA	Fine, i' faith'! Have you no modesty, no maiden shame, No touch of bashfulness? What, will you tear Impatient answers from my gentle tongue? Fie, fie, you counterfeit, you puppet, you!

285

HERMIA	Puppet? why so! Ay, that way goes the game. Now I perceive that she hath made compare Between our statures; she hath urged her height, And with her personage, her tall personage, Her height, forsooth, she hath prevailed with him.

290

3.2 The wood

Exchanging insults over their heights (Hermia is short, Helena tall), the women nearly come to blows.

Activities

Actors' interpretations: 'Why are you grown so rude?'

Write director's notes to lines 262–325 to help the actors playing Helena and Hermia. Give advice in answering the following questions:

- What is Helena's view of the situation by line 265? How does she interpret Hermia's and Lysander's behaviour?
- Which line shows Hermia that Lysander is serious about no longer loving her?
- How does Hermia say lines 282–284, and how does Helena react?
- Which of Helena's lines suggests that the exchange between the women has developed into an argument?
- How does Helena say line 317?
- What is Helena thinking and feeling by line 325?

296 **painted maypole** implying that Helena is wearing make-up and tall and skinny

300 **curst** bad-tempered and quarrelsome; exhibiting **shrewishness** (*line 301*)

302 **right** real, proper

307 **evermore** always

310 **stealth** secret escape

312 **chid me hence** told me angrily to go away

314 **so** so long as, provided that

317 **fond** foolish

323 **keen and shrewd** bitter and bad-tempered

324 **vixen** ferocious female

And are you grown so high in his esteem
Because I am so dwarfish and so low?   295
How low am I, thou painted maypole? Speak,
How low am I? I am not yet so low
But that my nails can reach unto thine eyes.

HELENA I pray you, though you mock me, gentlemen,
Let her not hurt me. I was never curst;   300
I have no gift at all in shrewishness;
I am a right maid for my cowardice;
Let her not strike me: you perhaps may think,
Because she is something lower than myself,
That I can match her.

HERMIA   'Lower'! hark, again!   305

HELENA Good Hermia, do not be so bitter with me.
I evermore did love you, Hermia,
Did ever keep your counsels, never wronged you;
Save that, in love unto Demetrius,
I told him of your stealth unto this wood.   310
He followed you; for love I followed him;
But he hath chid me hence and threatened me
To strike me, spurn me, nay, to kill me too.
And now, so you will let me quiet go,
To Athens will I bear my folly back,   315
And follow you no further. Let me go.
You see how simple and how fond I am.

HERMIA Why, get you gone! who is 't that hinders you?

HELENA A foolish heart, that I leave here behind.

HERMIA What, with Lysander?

HELENA   With Demetrius.   320

LYSANDER Be not afraid, she shall not harm thee, Helena.

DEMETRIUS No, sir, she shall not, though you take her part.

HELENA O, when she's angry, she is keen and shrewd.
She was a vixen when she went to school;
And though she be but little, she is fierce.   325

3.2 The wood

Hermia has had enough of being called 'little' and Helena has to run away to avoid being attacked. Meanwhile the men storm off together to decide their differences by fighting, and Hermia leaves, bewildered.

Activities

Shakespeare's language: Shakespearian insults

Look back through lines 257–330 and list the insults directed at Hermia. Divide them into insults which attack her for (a) clinging on to Lysander; and (b) her size.

Two of the insults refer to the fact that she is dark in colouring. Queen Elizabeth was very fair-skinned, with blonde, gingery hair, and this became the fashionable colouring for women. (Shakespeare wrote some of his sonnets to a woman known mysteriously as 'The Dark Lady', because of her complexion and hair colour.)

Re-read the two insults directed at Hermia's dark complexion (lines 257 and 263). Are they racist?

Invent some comparable insults which could be aimed at Helena because she is (a) tall and (b) fair-skinned and blonde. (There is already one on line 296.) Then improvise a scene in pairs in which all Shakespeare's 'short and dark' insults are answered by your invented 'tall and fair' insults.

327 **flout** mock, insult

329 **minimus** tiny thing

hindering knot-grass *weed which: (1) smothers other plants; (2) has a juice which stunts growth*

330 **bead** (1) small ornament; (2) something that hangs around the neck

330–331 **you are too officious … services** you are too keen to take the part of someone who doesn't want your help

335 **aby** pay for

336 **whose right … Helena** which of us has the greater right to Helena

337 **cheek by jowl** side-by-side, very closely (**jowl**: *loose skin on the throat*)

339 **coil** trouble

'long of because of, caused by

341 **curst** bad-tempered

342 **fray** fight

345 **thy negligence** your fault

still thou mistakest you are always making mistakes

346 **wilfully** deliberately

347 **shadows** (1) spirits and fairies; (2) darkness

350 **so far … enterprise** at least my action has been blameless to the extent that …

HERMIA   Little again? nothing but low and little?
         Why will you suffer her to flout me thus?
         Let me come to her.

LYSANDER   Get you gone, you dwarf,
         You minimus, of hindering knot-grass made,
         You bead, you acorn.

DEMETRIUS   You are too officious   330
         In her behalf that scorns your services.
         Let her alone; speak not of Helena;
         Take not her part. For if thou dost intend
         Never so little show of love to her,
         Thou shalt aby it.

LYSANDER   Now she holds me not.   335
         Now follow, if thou dar'st, to try whose right,
         Of thine or mine, is most in Helena.

DEMETRIUS   Follow? Nay, I'll go with thee cheek by jowl.

                              Exeunt LYSANDER *and* DEMETRIUS.

HERMIA   You, mistress, all this coil is 'long of you.
         Nay, go not back.

HELENA   I will not trust you, I   340
         Nor longer stay in your curst company.
         Your hands than mine are quicker for a fray,
         My legs are longer, though, to run away.

                                                        Exit.

HERMIA   I am amazed, and know not what to say.

                                                        Exit.

         OBERON *and* PUCK *come forward.*

OBERON   This is thy negligence; still thou mistak'st;   345
         Or else committ'st thy knaveries wilfully.

PUCK   Believe me, king of shadows, I mistook.
         Did not you tell me I should know the man
         By the Athenian garments he had on?
         And so far blameless proves my enterprise   350

3.2 The wood

Oberon rebukes Puck and orders him to ensure that the men avoid each other in the wood. When Puck has exhausted them and lulled them asleep, he is to squeeze an antidote juice on to Lysander's eyes. Meanwhile Oberon will get the changeling boy off Titania and then release her from the charm.

Activities

Actors' interpretations: tone of voice

How should Oberon and Puck say lines 345–353? Is Oberon angry, for example, or amused? Is Puck apologetic or delighted?

Aidan McArdle as Puck and Nicholas Jones as Oberon (RSC 1999)

Plot review (8): Puck's assignments

Imagine you are Oberon. Write a checklist for Puck, listing all the things he now has to do – and in the right order. Think carefully about how Puck might feel about these jobs and then, next to each one, write Puck's own scribbled comment (such as 'tough one, that' or 'this'll be fun').

351 **'nointed** anointed; placed the juice upon

352 **so sort** turn out in this way

353 **this their jangling ... sport** this arguing is my idea of fun

355 **Hie** hurry

356 **welkin** sky

357 **Acheron** *one of the rivers in the classical hell*

358 **testy** bad-tempered

359 **As** so that

360 **frame thy tongue** disguise your voice

361 **wrong** insult

362 **rail** speak insultingly

363 **look thou** make sure you

364 **death-counterfeiting** that looks like death

365 **batty** bat-like

369 **wonted** familiar

372 **wend** go

373 **league whose date** alliance whose duration

376 **charméd** bewitched

380 **Aurora's harbinger** *the fore-runner of the dawn (the morning star)*

382 **damnéd spirits** the ghosts of the dead

383 **crossways** *People who had committed suicide were buried at crossroads.*

387 **for aye** for ever

That I have 'nointed an Athenian's eyes;
And so far am I glad it so did sort,
As this their jangling I esteem a sport.

OBERON   Thou seest these lovers seek a place to fight.
Hie, therefore, Robin, overcast the night;   355
The starry welkin cover thou anon
With drooping fog as black as Acheron;
And lead these testy rivals so astray
As one come not within another's way.
Like to Lysander sometime frame thy tongue,   360
Then stir Demetrius up with bitter wrong;
And sometime rail thou like Demetrius;
And from each other look thou lead them thus,
Till o'er their brows death-counterfeiting sleep
With leaden legs and batty wings doth creep;   365
Then crush this herb into Lysander's eye;
Whose liquor hath this virtuous property,
To take from thence all error with his might
And make his eyeballs roll with wonted sight.
When they next wake, all this derision   370
Shall seem a dream, and fruitless vision;
And back to Athens shall the lovers wend,
With league whose date till death shall never end.
Whiles I in this affair do thee employ,
I'll to my Queen, and beg her Indian boy;   375
And then I will her charméd eye release
From monster's view, and all things shall be peace.

PUCK   My fairy lord, this must be done with haste,
For night's swift dragons cut the clouds full fast,
And yonder shines Aurora's harbinger;   380
At whose approach, ghosts wandering here and there,
Troop home to churchyards. Damnéd spirits all,
That in crossways and floods have burial,
Already to their wormy beds are gone;
For fear lest day should look their shames upon,   385
They wilfully themselves exile from light,
And must for aye consort with black-browed night.

OBERON   But we are spirits of another sort:
I with the morning's love have oft made sport,
And, like a forester, the groves may tread   390

3.2 The wood

Puck keeps the men apart and leads them astray by imitating their voices.

Activities

Themes: dreams

'Shall seem a dream, and fruitless vision'
Oberon tells Puck that, when Bottom and
the lovers wake up, their experiences in
the wood 'Shall seem a dream, and
fruitless vision' (line 371).

In pairs, look back through the play and
make a note of anything which suggests
that we, the audience, have been
watching a dream:

- Which events in the story might have
  come straight out of a dream, for
  example?
- Which visions created by the language
  seem particularly dream-like and
  surreal?
- Have any of the events or the
  language of the play reminded you of
  dreams that you have had?

When you have discussed these
questions, create a collage to represent
the dream world of the play. You could
use images cut from magazines, your
own artwork and lines from the script.

389–393 **I with ... streams** *Oberon can
stay in this world during
daylight hours.*

392 **Neptune** (*Roman god of*) the
sea (*see page 170*)

394 **notwithstanding** despite that

402 **drawn** with my sword drawn

403 **straight** immediately

404 **plainer** more open (*or:* more
level)

408 **thou look'st for wars** you're
looking for a fight

409 **recreant** coward

410 **defiled** disgraced

Even till the eastern gate, all fiery-red,
Opening on Neptune, with fair blessèd beams
Turns into yellow gold his salt green streams.
But notwithstanding, haste, make no delay:
We may effect this business yet ere day.   395

Exit OBERON.

PUCK   Up and down, up and down,
I will lead them up and down;
I am feared in field and town;
Goblin, lead them up and down.
Here comes one.   400

Enter LYSANDER.

LYSANDER   Where art thou, proud Demetrius? Speak thou now.

PUCK   (*as* DEMETRIUS)
Here villain, drawn and ready. Where art thou?

LYSANDER   I will be with thee straight.

PUCK   (*as* DEMETRIUS)
                                        Follow me, then,
To plainer ground.

Exit LYSANDER.

Enter DEMETRIUS.

DEMETRIUS   Lysander, speak again;
Thou runaway, thou coward, art thou fled?   405
Speak! In some bush? Where dost thou hide thy
      head?

PUCK   (*as* LYSANDER)
Thou coward, art thou bragging to the stars,
Telling the bushes that thou look'st for wars,
And wilt not come? Come, recreant, come, thou
      child;
I'll whip thee with a rod. He is defiled   410
That draws a sword on thee.

DEMETRIUS   Yea, art thou there?

3.2 The wood

Exhausted by their fruitless chasing around the forest, Lysander and Demetrius are led into the clearing by Puck and lie down to sleep. Soon Helena joins them.

Activities

Plot review (9): surveying 3.2

3.2 is a long scene. To remind yourself of what has happened, work in groups to produce a silent movie version. Decide which main events you are going to show and then draw up caption cards to help the audience understand what is going on (such as 'Oberon sprinkles the love-juice on Demetrius's eyes'). Finally, rehearse the scene and perform it to other groups. Try to find some suitable silent-movie piano music to accompany the actions (which might be made jerky and speeded-up).

Actors' interpretations: 'And here will rest me ...'

Lysander is the first of the four lovers to enter and collapse in exhaustion. Is his tiredness natural, or suddenly inflicted upon him by one of Puck's spells? (Look back at the activity on page 72.) Try acting it out both ways and see which you prefer. (Which version fits your interpretation of the play?)

412 **we'll try ... here** this isn't the place to prove that we're men (*by fighting*)

417 **That** so that

420 **spite** injury

422 **Abide** wait for

wot know

426 **buy this dear** pay dearly for this

428 **constraineth** forces

430 **look** expect

432 **Abate thy hours** make your hours seem shorter

PUCK   (*as* LYSANDER)
Follow my voice; we'll try no manhood here.

Exeunt.

Re-enter LYSANDER.

LYSANDER   He goes before me, and still dares me on;
When I come where he calls, then he is gone.
The villain is much lighter-heeled than I: 415
I followed fast, but faster he did fly,
That fallen am I in dark uneven way,
And here will rest me. Come, thou gentle day;

Lies down.

For if but once thou show me thy grey light,
I'll find Demetrius, and revenge this spite. (*Sleeps*)   420

Re-enter PUCK *and* DEMETRIUS.

PUCK   (*as* LYSANDER)
Ho, ho, ho! coward, why com'st thou not?

DEMETRIUS   Abide me, if thou dar'st; for well I wot,
Thou runn'st before me, shifting every place,
And dar'st not stand, nor look me in the face.
Where art thou now?

PUCK   (*as* LYSANDER)
                   Come hither, I am here.   425

DEMETRIUS   Nay, then, thou mock'st me; thou shalt buy this dear,
If ever I thy face by daylight see.
Now, go thy way: faintness constraineth me
To measure out my length on this cold bed:
By day's approach look to be visited.   430

Lies down and sleeps.

Enter HELENA.

HELENA   O weary night, O long and tedious night,
Abate thy hours, shine comforts from the east,
That I may back to Athens by daylight.

3.2 The wood

Hermia enters, dishevelled, and falls asleep with the others. Puck squeezes the antidote on to Lysander's eyes, so that he will return to his love for Hermia when he awakes.

Activities

Actors' interpretations: enter the lovers …

Look back at the second activity on page 94. Then use the stage plans on page 168 to 'block' lines 413–447 (work out the actors' moves and plot them on a diagram). Finally, act out the sequence. A number of things will need careful planning and practice, including:
- entrances and exits for Lysander and Demetrius
- Puck's movements, as he lures the men in different directions
- imitating Lysander's and Demetrius's voices.

Plot review (10): the lovers

Who loves whom?
Look back at the activities on pages 46 and 76. Now draw up a Phase 4 version of your lovers' diagram, showing who will love whom when they wake up, now that Puck has anointed Lysander's eyes.

439 **curst** bad tempered
440 **knavish** mischievous
443 **Bedabbled** splashed
447 **fray** fight
461 **Jack … Jill** *the boy will get his girl: couples will be properly paired up*

From these that my poor company detest;
And sleep, that sometimes shuts up sorrow's eye,   435
Steal me awhile from mine own company.

Lies down and sleeps.

PUCK   Yet but three? Come one more.
Two of both kinds makes up four.
Here she comes, curst and sad;
Cupid is a knavish lad,   440
Thus to make poor females mad.

Enter HERMIA.

HERMIA   Never so weary, never so in woe,
Bedabbled with the dew, and torn with briers,
I can no further crawl, no further go;
My legs can keep no pace with my desires.   445
Here will I rest me till the break of day.
Heavens shield Lysander, if they mean a fray!

Lies down and sleeps.

PUCK   On the ground
Sleep sound;
I'll apply   450
To your eye,
Gentle lover, remedy. (*Squeezes the juice on* LYSANDER's
eyes)
When thou wak'st,
Thou tak'st
True delight   455
In the sight
Of thy former lady's eye;
And the country proverb known,
That every man should take his own,
In your waking shall be shown.   460
Jack shall have Jill;
Nought shall go ill;
The man shall have his mare again, and all shall be
well.

Exit.

The lovers lie asleep.

Exam practice

Character review: Bottom (4)

His humour and personality
In 3.1, Bottom first gives advice to the other mechanicals about their play, and is then ensnared by Puck's magic.

What do you learn about Bottom and how does his character add to the humour in 3.1?

Before you begin to write you should think about:
- the points that Bottom makes about 'Pyramus and Thisby' and the suggestions he puts forward
- his reactions when the others run away
- his response to the appearance of Titania
- his words to the other fairies.

Plot review (11): the lovers

Who loves whom now?
Update the changing record of who-loves-whom with a diagram for Phase 4 (to represent how things will be when they wake up).

Character review: Puck (4)

His powers and qualities
Think about Puck's magic powers. In each case:
1. Look back at the following moments when Puck's magic powers are described or seen in action:
   - 2.1.32–57
   - 2.1.175–176
   - 3.1.76–109
   - 3.2.6–40
   - 3.2.100–101
   - 3.2.388–395
   - 3.2.396–463.
2. Where else do you think his magic might be seen in a performance, even though it is not described in the script? Look at the lovers falling asleep at the end of 3.2, for example.
3. What do the following moments suggest about the kinds of magic power that Puck does *not* possess?
   - 2.1.155
   - 2.2.65–82, 3.2.42, 3.2.88–91 and 3.2.345–347
4. Which of the powers you have listed are beneficial to human beings and which are a nuisance? Are there any that you cannot decide about?
5. Which of his acts of magic seem to give him most pleasure? What kind of pleasure is it?

6. Grade each of the following words or phrases from 1 (disagree) to 5 (agree) as accurate descriptions of Puck as you see him. Find moments in the play to support your grading in each case:
   - mischievous
   - irresponsible
   - malicious
   - child-like
   - all-powerful
   - despises mortals.

   Think up further words to describe him and write a 'Puck' poem.

Theme: love (9)

What effect does the juice have?

Puck anoints Lysander's eyes with the antidote and the lovers are happily paired up. Demetrius, of course, is still under the influence of the love-juice. Does this mean that 'the course of true love' is only running smoothly because of the artificial influence of fairy magic? Or can we believe that all the disruption and the final sorting out might have happened anyway in the normal course of events – and that all the fairies have done is to speed things up? Hold a class discussion to explore this important question.

Character review: Bottom (5)

His disappearance

A In pairs, recap on exactly what happened to Bottom and how the rest of the mechanicals reacted to Puck's magic.

Imagine that Peter Quince comes on to Radio Athens to discuss Bottom's disappearance and appeal for information concerning his whereabouts. In pairs, improvise the interview. Firstly, the interviewer might introduce the story with details on:
- who Bottom is (his full name, address, job, age, usual appearance ...)
- why his friends need to contact him urgently (they are rehearsing an important play ...).

B Then Peter Quince might be asked questions about:
- Bottom's personality
- the last time he was seen
- what exactly happened in the wood
- what Bottom's current appearance is
- what he fears might have happened to Bottom
- why it is so important to get him back soon.

C Write a scene in which the remaining mechanicals return to Peter Quince's house, discuss what they saw, speculate on what might have happened and express their concern (both for Bottom's safety and their chances of performing the play). Look back through earlier scenes and activities to ensure that each character behaves and speaks appropriately.

4.1 The wood

Titania leads Bottom in and she caresses him while the fairies scratch his hairy head.

Activities

Actors' interpretations: in Titania's bower

At the end of 3.1, after Titania had fallen in love with Bottom, she told her fairies 'lead him to my bower' (line 192). What do we suppose they have been up to?

A number of teachers who took young children to the 1999 RSC production complained because they felt it was too sexually explicit (too open in showing that Bottom and Titania were having a sexual relationship). Is the relationship between Bottom and Titania a sexual one, in your opinion? What evidence is there to suggest that it is, or isn't? If it is, should it be made explicit?

Write director's notes to describe how the characters enter at the beginning of this scene. What do they look like? How do they behave with each other? What kind of relationship do they convey to the audience?

2 **amiable** lovable

coy caress

10 **Monsieur** *Bottom's attempt at 'posh', gentlemanly speech; later he tries* **signior** *(line 17) and* **cavalery** *(line 23).*

20 **neaf** fist

21 **leave your curtsy** don't bother to remove your hat out of respect (**curtsy** = courtesy)

23 **Cavalery** *Bottom's pronunciation of 'cavalier' (see line 10), meaning knight*

Act 4

Scene 1

The same place.

Enter TITANIA *and* BOTTOM, *with the* Fairies *attending, and* OBERON *behind, unseen.*

TITANIA   Come, sit thee down upon this flowery bed,
While I thy amiable cheeks do coy,
And stick musk-roses in thy sleek smooth head,
And kiss thy fair large ears, my gentle joy.

BOTTOM   Where's Peaseblossom?   5

PEASE-BLOSSOM   Ready.

BOTTOM   Scratch my head, Peaseblossom. Where's Monsieur Cobweb?

COBWEB   Ready.

BOTTOM   Monsieur Cobweb, good monsieur, get you your   10
weapons in your hand, and kill me a red-hipped
humble-bee on the top of a thistle; and good
monsieur, bring me the honey-bag. Do not fret
yourself too much in the action, monsieur; and
good monsieur, have a care the honey-bag break   15
not; I would be loth to have you overflown with a
honey-bag, signior. Where's Monsieur
Mustardseed?

MUSTARD-SEED   Ready.

BOTTOM   Give my your neaf, Monsieur Mustardseed. Pray   20
you, leave your curtsy, good monsieur.

MUSTARD-SEED   What's your will?

BOTTOM   Nothing, good monsieur, but to help Cavalery
Cobmeb to scratch. I must to the barber's,
monsieur, for methinks I am marvellous hairy   25
about the face. And I am such a tender ass, if my
hair do but tickle me, I must scratch.

4.1 The wood

Bottom gives some final instructions to the fairies and dozes off. Oberon enters with Puck to find Titania and Bottom asleep.

Activities

Actors' interpretations: Bottom the ass

Look back at the activity on page 62 about Bottom's braying. What does Bottom say and do in this scene (4.1) to underline the joke that he has been transformed into an ass but does not realise?

- What references are there in the script to suggest that Bottom looks like and behaves like an ass?
- What actions might the actor perform to bring out Bottom's ass-like qualities? (Think especially about voice and movement.)
- Should the actor be wearing a full ass's head or something which still reveals his human face? (Look at the photographs on pages 68 and 104.)
- Should his bodily shape have been transformed in any way?

Act out lines 1–45, putting into practice as many of your ideas as you can.

30 **the tongs and the bones** crude musical instruments: *tongs were struck like a triangle; bones were clicked together in pairs*

32 **peck of provender** a good weight of food

34 **bottle** small bundle

hath no fellow there's nothing like it

39 **exposition** *he means 'disposition' (an inclination)*

40 **all ways** in all directions

47 **dotage** infatuation (*for Bottom*)

48 **of late** recently

49 **favours** *love-tokens to give Bottom*

hateful repulsive

50 **upbraid** scold

53–56 **And that ... bewail** the same dew which usually swells like pearls, now hung in the flowers' eyes like tears weeping for their own disgrace

57 **at my pleasure** as much as I liked

TITANIA	What, wilt thou hear some music, my sweet love?
BOTTOM	I have a reasonable good ear in music. Let's have the tongs and the bones. 30
TITANIA	Or say, sweet love, what thou desirest to eat.
BOTTOM	Truly, a peck of provender; I could munch your good dry oats. Methinks I have a great desire to a bottle of hay: good hay, sweet hay, hath no fellow.
TITANIA	I have a venturous fairy, that shall seek 35 The squirrel's hoard, and fetch thee new nuts.
BOTTOM	I had rather have a handful or two of dried peas. But I pray you, let none of your people stir me; I have an exposition of sleep come upon me.
TITANIA	Sleep thou, and I will wind thee in my arms. 40 Fairies, be gone, and be all ways away.

Exeunt Fairies.

So doth the woodbine the sweet honeysuckle
Gently entwist; the female ivy so
Enrings the barky fingers of the elm.
O, how I love thee! how I dote on thee!   45

They sleep.

Enter PUCK.

OBERON	(*coming forward*) Welcome, good Robin: seest thou this sweet sight? Her dotage now I do begin to pity; For meeting her of late behind the wood, Seeking sweet favours for this hateful fool, I did upbraid her, and fall out with her. 50 For she his hairy temples then had rounded With coronet of fresh and fragrant flowers; And that same dew, which sometime on the buds Was wont to swell like round and orient pearls, Stood now within the pretty flowerets' eyes 55 Like tears that did their own disgrace bewail. When I had at my pleasure taunted her,

4.1 The wood

Oberon tells Puck that Titania has handed over the changeling boy and that he now feels some pity for her. He removes the charm, awakes her and, as Puck takes the ass's head off Bottom, the King and Queen of the fairies are reconciled.

Activities

Character review: Oberon (3)

His reactions
How do you think Oberon felt as he watched Titania with Bottom (lines 1–45)? Might he have felt amused; jealous; superior? (Your answer will depend partly on your response to the questions posed in the activity on page 100.)

Re-read lines 48–61 and improvise the meeting that Oberon describes. Think about his feelings as you decide how he ought to react during the scene.

Clare Higgins as Titania, John Carlisle as Oberon and David Troughton as Bottom (RSC 1989)

59 **changeling child** *see 2.1.20–27 and 120–145*

60 **straight** straightaway

63 **hateful imperfection** *the effect of the love-juice*

64 **scalp** head

65 **swain** young lover

66 **other** others (*the lovers*)

67 **May all … repair** they may all return to Athens

69 **fierce vexation** wild agitation, troubling visions

71 **as thou wast wont** as you used

73 **Dian's bud** *The herb which will act as an antidote (see 2.1.184 and 3.2.366); perhaps artemisia (Artemis being the Greek name for Diana, goddess of chastity; see page 170).*

77 **enamoured of** in love with

79 **visage** face

81–82 **and strike … sense** *Oberon deadens the senses of Bottom and the lovers.*

87 **new in amity** friends once again

And she in mild terms begged my patience,
I then did ask of her her changeling child;
Which straight she gave me, and her fairy sent   60
To bear him to my bower in fairy land.
And now I have the boy, I will undo
This hateful imperfection of her eyes.
And, gentle Puck, take this transforméd scalp,
From off the head of this Athenian swain,   65
That he awaking when the other do,
May all to Athens back again repair,
And think no more of this night's accidents
But as the fierce vexation of a dream.
But first I will release the Fairy Queen.   70

Touches TITANIA's *eyelids.*

Be as thou wast wont to be;
See as thou wast wont to see.
Dian's bud o'er Cupid's flower
Hath such force and blessed power.
Now, my Titania, wake you, my sweet Queen.   75

TITANIA   (*wakes and rises*)
My Oberon! What visions have I seen!
Methought I was enamoured of an ass.

OBERON   There lies your love.

TITANIA   How came these things to pass?
O, how mine eyes do loathe his visage now!

OBERON   Silence awhile. Robin, take off this head;   80
Titania, music call, and strike more dead
Than common sleep, of all these five the sense.

TITANIA   Music, ho music, such as charmeth sleep!

Music plays.

PUCK   Now, when thou wak'st, with thine own fool's eyes
peep.

OBERON   Sound, music; come, my Queen take hands with me, 85
And rock the ground whereon these sleepers be.
Now thou and I are new in amity,

4.1 The wood

Puck warns Oberon that dawn has broken, and as the fairies leave, Theseus enters with Hippolyta and Egeus. They are hunting and discuss the merits of their hounds.

Activities

Character review: Titania

Her dream

Write the conversation (in your own words or a language echoing Shakespeare's) in which Titania tells Oberon about the strange events she recollects since she fell asleep at the beginning of 2.2, and he gradually reveals to her exactly what happened.

Shakespeare's language: Oberon's changing mood

Copy and complete this chart to help you compare the language of Oberon here (lines 87–92) with his language during the Act 2 confrontation with Titania (2.1.60–147):

	2.1	4.1
(a) Changes in the verse	*no rhyme*	*rhyme example:* ....
(b) Changes in vocabulary	*harsh, violent words*	*peaceful words*
examples:	....	....

What is the effect of these differences?

88 **solemnly** ceremoniously, formally

93 **attend and mark** listen and take notice

95 **sad** serious

97 **compass** circle

104 **observation** May morning ceremonies

105 **since we … day** since it is still early

107 **Uncouple** unleash the hounds

108 **Dispatch** get it done

110–111 **mark the … conjunction** listen to the combined sounds of the hounds and the echo

112 **Hercules and Cadmus** *legendary Greek heroes (see page 170)*

113 **bayed** cornered (*the bear was 'at bay'*)

114 **Sparta** *a city in Greece; 'Spartan' meant extremely tough and courageous*

115 **gallant chiding** fine baying

117 **mutual** common (*everything seemed to be making the same sound*)

118 **So musical a discord** *an example of oxymoron, where the words seem at first to be contradicting each other*

And will tomorrow midnight solemnly
Dance in Duke Theseus' house triumphantly,
And bless it to all fair prosperity.   90
There shall the pairs of faithful lovers be
Wedded, with Theseus, all in jollity.

PUCK   Fairy King, attend and mark;
              I do hear the morning lark.

OBERON   Then, my Queen, in silence sad   95
              Trip we after the night's shade;
              We the globe can compass soon,
              Swifter than the wandering moon.

TITANIA   Come, my lord, and in our flight
              Tell me how it came this night   100
              That I sleeping here was found,
              With these mortals on the ground.

Exeunt. The lovers *and* BOTTOM *sleep on.*

Hunting horns sound. Enter THESEUS, HIPPOLYTA, EGEUS, *and their train.*

THESEUS   Go one of you, find out the forester,
              For now our observation is performed;
              And since we have the vaward of the day,   105
              My love shall hear the music of my hounds.
              Uncouple in the western valley; let them go;
              Dispatch, I say, and find the forester.

Exit an Attendant.

              We will, fair queen, up to the mountain's top,
              And mark the musical confusion   110
              Of hounds and echo in conjunction.

HIPPOLYTA   I was with Hercules and Cadmus once,
              When in a wood of Crete they bayed the bear
              With hounds of Sparta; never did I hear
              Such gallant chiding; for, besides the groves, 115
              The skies, the fountains, every region near
              Seemed all one mutual cry. I never heard
              So musical a discord, such sweet thunder.

THESEUS   My hounds are bred out of the Spartan kind,

4.1 The wood

Suddenly Theseus notices the lovers asleep on the ground and recalls that this is the day when Hermia is required to make her decision. He orders them to be woken up.

Activities

Plot review (12): Hermia's choice

1. In pairs, re-read 1.1.117–121 and remind yourselves of the 'choice' that faces Hermia. What decision is she supposed to make today?
2. As you watch the play, does it worry you that trouble might be brewing to destroy Hermia's happiness? Or do you feel that matters will now be sorted out?
3. Write down Hermia's thoughts from the moment she wakes up (line 139) to the end of Egeus's speech (line 159).

Themes: love (10)

Theseus and Hippolyta
Look back at the opening of the play and re-read the exchanges between Theseus and Hippolyta. Then, in pairs, act out 4.1.103–127, first as though the couple are deeply in love and she is genuinely fascinated to hear about his hounds; then as though Theseus is one of those people who always have to go one better and is irritating Hippolyta with his bragging.

Try a third interpretation of your own and decide which one fits your overall interpretation of these characters.

120 **so flewed, so sanded** with the same chaps (*skin hanging from the cheek*) and the same sandy colour

122 **Crook-kneed ... bulls** with bent knees and with skin hanging from the throat (**dewlapped**) like bulls from Thessaly (*in Greece*)

123–124 **matched in ... each** their barks were in tune, like a peal of bells

125 **holla'd to** called after by the huntsmen (*who shout 'holla'*)

131 **of** at

134 **in grace ... solemnity** to grace our ceremony

139–140 **Saint Valentine ... couple** *People believed that birds chose their mates on Saint Valentine's Day.*

143 **gentle concord** peaceful agreement

144 **jealousy** mistrust

151 **hither** here

So flewed, so sanded, and their heads are hung 120
With ears that sweep away the morning dew,
Crook-kneed and dew-lapped, like Thessalian bulls;
Slow in pursuit, but matched in mouth like bells,
Each under each. A cry more tuneable
Was never holla'd to, nor cheered with horn, 125
In Crete, in Sparta, nor in Thessaly.
Judge when you hear. But soft, what nymphs are
     these?

EGEUS   My lord, this is my daughter here asleep,
And this Lysander, this Demetrius is,
This Helena, old Nedar's Helena; 130
I wonder of their being here together.

THESEUS No doubt they rose up early to observe
The rite of May; and, hearing our intent,
Came here in grace of our solemnity.
But speak, Egeus; is not this the day 135
That Hermia should give answer of her choice?

EGEUS   It is, my lord.

THESEUS Go bid the huntsmen wake them with their horns.

Horns sound. A shout within. The lovers wake up.

Good morrow, friends! Saint Valentine is past:
Begin these wood-birds but to couple now? 140

LYSANDER Pardon, my lord.

The lovers kneel.

THESEUS   I pray you all, stand up
I know you two are rival enemies.
How comes this gentle concord in the world,
That hatred is so far from jealousy
To sleep by hate, and fear no enmity? 145

LYSANDER My lord, I shall reply amazédly,
Half sleep, half waking. But as yet, I swear,
I cannot truly say how I came her.
But as I think, for truly would I speak,
And now I do bethink me, so it is: 150
I came with Hermia hither: our intent

4.1 The wood

When Lysander admits that he and Hermia had planned to elope, Egeus demands that he should be punished. But Demetrius declares his new-found love for Helena, and Theseus decides that the two pairs of lovers can marry on the same day as he and Hippolyta.

Activities

Character review: Theseus (2)

'Egeus, I will overbear your will ...'
Improvise a conversation back in Athens in which Theseus explains to Egeus why he overruled his wishes and Egeus expresses his own views on the matter.

Character review: Egeus

Daughter problems
Look back over Egeus's two scripted appearances (in 1.1 and this scene). Then write a letter from Egeus to a relative in which he recounts the problems he has had with his daughter and then describes today's developments.

- Had he realised that Hermia had run away?
- What does he feel about Theseus's decision to override his (Egeus's) wishes? (Shakespeare doesn't give him any lines after that point.)
- What might still be puzzling him about the whole situation?
- Does he have views on 'the younger generation' generally?

Bring out what you know about Egeus's character in the way he writes the letter and the opinions he expresses.

157 **Thereby** in that way

160 **stealth** secret escape

161 **their purpose hither** their purpose in coming here

163 **in fancy** motivated by love

164 **I wot not** I do not know

167 **idle gaud** worthless toy

172 **betrothed** engaged to be married

173–174 **like in sickness ... taste** just as people hate certain foods when they are ill, but regain their normal taste when they recover

175–176 **it** *'the food' (from line 173–174); i.e. Helena*

179 **overbear your will** overrule your wishes

182 **for ... worn** because the morning is nearly over

185 **in great solemnity** very ceremoniously

187 **undistinguishable** difficult to make out

Was to be gone from Athens, where we might,
Without the peril of the Athenian law –

EGEUS   Enough, enough, my lord; you have enough;
          I beg the law, the law, upon his head.   155
          They would have stolen away; they would,
              Demetrius,
          Thereby to have defeated you and me:
          You of your wife, and me of my consent;
          Of my consent, that she should be your wife.

DEMETRIUS My lord, fair Helen told me of their stealth,   160
          Of this their purpose hither to this wood,
          And I in fury hither followed them;
          Fair Helena in fancy following me.
          But, my good lord, I wot not by what power,
          But by some power it is, my love to Hermia,   165
          Melted as doth the snow, seems to me now
          As the remembrance of an idle gaud,
          Which in my childhood I did dote upon;
          And all the faith, the virtue of my heart,
          The object and the pleasure of mine eye,   170
          Is only Helena. To her, my lord,
          Was I betrothed ere I saw Hermia;
          But like in sickness did I loathe this food;
          But, as in health, come to my natural taste,
          Now I do wish it, love it, long for it,   175
          And will for evermore be true to it.

THESEUS   Fair lovers, you are fortunately met;
          Of this discourse we more will hear anon.
          Egeus, I will overbear your will,
          For in the temple, by and by, with us   180
          These couples shall eternally be knit.
          And, for the morning now is something worn,
          Our purposed hunting shall be set aside.
          Away with us to Athens; three and three,
          We'll hold a feast in great solemnity.   185
          Come, Hippolyta.

                    Exeunt all but the lovers *and* BOTTOM, *still asleep.*

DEMETRIUS These things seem small and undistinguishable,
          Like far-off mountains turnéd into clouds.

4.1 The wood

Left alone, the four lovers try to make some sense of their strange experience, and wonder if they have been dreaming. Deciding that they are indeed awake, they follow Theseus back to Athens. Bottom wakes up and recalls the most extraordinary dream.

Activities

Character review: the lovers (3)

'And by the way let us recount our dreams'
In fours, improvise the conversation that the lovers have as they return to Athens. What are the main events that they recall? What will they still be puzzled about? What questions will they want to ask each other?

Shakespeare's language: mixed senses

Bottom and Quince frequently get their senses confused (see 3.1.90). What did Bottom mean to say in lines 210–213? Write a few lines of your own in which Quince confuses his senses as he tries to describe the amazing events of Bottom's transformation in 3.1.

Bottom (Des Barrit) in the 1994 RSC production

189 **with parted eye** with one eye out of focus with the other

194 **yet** still

201 **Heigh-ho!** *Bottom yawns.*

205 **wit** intelligence

206 **expound** explain

209 **but a patched fool** nothing better than a jester (*wearing a patchwork costume*)

212 **conceive** imagine

214 **a ballad** *strange happenings were frequently turned into ballads*

215–216 **it hath no bottom** (1) it is fathomless; you can't get to the bottom of it; (2) it isn't based upon anything real

216 **in the latter end** towards the end

217 **Peradventure** perhaps

218 **gracious** appealing

HERMIA	Methinks I see these things with parted eye,
	When every thing seems double.

HELENA	So methinks;	190
	And I have found Demetrius, like a jewel,	
	Mine own, and not mine own.	

DEMETRIUS	Are you sure	
	That we are awake? It seems to me	
	That yet we sleep, we dream. Do not you think	
	The Duke was here, and bid us follow him?	195

HERMIA	Yea, and my father.

HELENA	And Hippolyta.

LYSANDER	And he did bid us follow to the temple.

DEMETRIUS	Why then, we are awake; let's follow him,
	And by the way let us recount our dreams.

Exeunt the lovers.

BOTTOM	(*waking up*)

When my cue comes, call me, and I will answer. My 200
next is 'Most fair Pyramus'. Heigh-ho! Peter Quince!
Flute the bellows-mender! Snout the tinker!
Starveling! God's my life! Stolen hence, and left me
asleep! I have had a most rare vision. I have had
a dream, past the wit of man to say what dream it 205
was. Man is but an ass if he go about to expound
this dream. Methought I was – there is no man can
tell what. Methought I was, and methought I had
– but man is but a patched fool, if he will offer to
say what methought I had. The eye of man hath 210
not heard, the ear of man hath not seen, man's
hand is not able to taste, his tongue to conceive,
nor his heart to report, what my dream was. I will
get Peter Quince to write a ballad of this dream; it
shall be called 'Bottom's Dream', because it hath 215
no bottom; and I will sing it in the latter end of a
play, before the Duke. Peradventure, to make it
the more gracious, I shall sing it at her death.

Exit.

4.2 Peter Quince's house

The other mechanicals are despondent at Bottom's continued absence; without him, the play cannot go on. As they are bemoaning the loss of the money the Duke would have given them, Bottom arrives.

Activities

Actors' interpretations: the mechanicals' changing moods

In groups of six, act out lines 1–27, bringing out (a) the mechanicals' utter disappointment and misery (line 1–24); and (b) their joy and amazement when Bottom turns up.

Paul Webster as Quince and Dhebi Oparei as Starveling (RSC 1989)

4 **transported** (1) carried off; (2) magically turned into something else

8 **discharge** perform the part of

9 **wit** talent, skill

11 **person** appearance

12 **paramour** *He means 'paragon' (an example of perfection); a paramour is an adulterous lover.*

14 **thing of naught** immoral person

18 **we had … men** our fortunes would have been made

19 **sweet bully Bottom!** dear, good old Bottom!

19–20 **sixpence a day** *The weekly pension which might have been given to him by the Duke. (As an idea of what this would have been worth, a joiner like Snug would have earned eight pence a day.)*

21 **An** if

24 **in** for

26 **courageous** wonderful

4.2

Scene 2

Athens.

Enter QUINCE, FLUTE, SNOUT, *and* STARVELING.

QUINCE   Have you sent to Bottom's house? Is he come
              home yet?

STARVELING   He cannot be heard of. Out of doubt he is
              transported.

FLUTE   If he come not, then the play is marred. It goes not   5
              forward, doth it?

QUINCE   It is not possible: you have not a man in all Athens
              able to discharge Pyramus, but he.

FLUTE   No; he hath simply the best wit of any handicraft
              man in Athens.   10

QUINCE   Yea, and the best person too; and he is a very
              paramour for a sweet voice.

FLUTE   You must say 'paragon'. A paramour is, God bless
              us, a thing of naught.

Enter SNUG.

SNUG   Masters! the Duke is coming from the temple, and   15
              there is two or three lords and ladies more
              married. If our sport had gone forward, we had
              all been made men.

FLUTE   O sweet bully Bottom! Thus hath he lost sixpence
              a day during his life; he could not have scaped   20
              sixpence a day. An the Duke had not given him
              sixpence a day for playing Pyramus, I'll be
              hanged. He would have deserved it: Sixpence a
              day in Pyramus, or nothing.

Enter BOTTOM.

BOTTOM   Where are these lads? Where are these hearts?   25

QUINCE   Bottom! O, most courageous day! O, most happy
              hour!

4.2 Peter Quince's house

The mechanicals are delighted to see Bottom, who refuses to tell them of his experiences, but does instruct them to get all their apparel together and prepare themselves because their play has been put forward as a possible entertainment for the Duke's wedding.

Activities

Character review: Bottom (6)

'Not a word of me ...'
Re-read lines 28–32. Twice Bottom promises to tell them what happened and each time he fails to do so. From what you know of his character and also the magical experiences he has undergone, do you think that (a) he is deliberately tormenting his friends by exciting their curiosity and then not satisfying it; or (b) he is genuinely trying to tell them what happened but finds that he is incapable of putting into words (or even recalling it at all); or (c) there is a different interpretation?

Act out the different interpretations and decide which you prefer. Which one best fits your view of what happened to him in the wood?

28 **discourse** talk about, recount

33 **apparel** costumes

34 **strings** *to tie the false beards on*

34–35 **new ribbons to your pumps** new laces for your shoes

35 **presently** immediately

37 **preferred** put forward (*as we see in 5.1.42–43, it has been short-listed*)

41 **sweet breath** (1) sweet-smelling breath; (2) sweet-sounding words

BOTTOM	Masters, I am to discourse wonders; but ask me not what, for if I tell you, I am no true Athenian. I will tell you everything right as it fell out. 30
QUINCE	Let us hear, sweet Bottom.
BOTTOM	Not a word of me: all that I will tell you is, that the Duke hath dined. Get your apparel together, good strings to your beards, new ribbons to your pumps, meet presently at the palace; every man 35 look o'er his part; for the short and the long is, our play is preferred. In any case, let Thisby have clean linen: and let not him that plays the lion pare his nails, for they shall hang out for the lion's claws. And, most dear actors, eat no onions, 40 nor garlic; for we are to utter sweet breath, and I do not doubt but to hear them say, it is a sweet comedy. No more words: away, go away!

Exeunt.

Exam practice

Character review: Hippolyta

Her diary
In 4.1 Hippolyta goes hunting with Theseus and they find the lovers asleep. Imagine you are Hippolyta. Write your diary entry for that day, in which you record the discovery of the lovers and write about your feelings.

Before you begin to write, you should think about:
- how Hippolyta felt about the conversation concerning hounds (look back at the activity on page 108)
- what she felt about Theseus's decision to overrule Egeus (lines 179–181)
- whether she is pleased or upset that Theseus cancelled the hunt (lines 182–183)
- whether she is looking forward to being married to Theseus
- whether her views about him have changed since the beginning of the play.

Character review: the mechanicals (3)

Getting ready
In groups of six, improvise a scene in which the mechanicals meet to decide what final preparations need to be made before performing the play. Make sure that you all remain 'in character' (speaking and behaving as your individual mechanical would do), and that you solve any problems which arise in typical 'mechanical' fashion.

Themes: love (11)

'The course of true love ...'

A List each of the pairs of lovers in the play. What difficulties have they had to overcome before they can get married?

B Demetrius draws a distinction between 'doting' (4.1.168) and loving. Look back through the play and list examples of behaviour which, in your opinion:
(a) demonstrate genuine love
(b) can be described as infatuation or doting
(c) suggest that the 'love' is built on shaky foundations and might not last.

Remember that this is all a matter of opinion and interpretation.

C How successful do you think each of the three marriages will be? In pairs, freeze-frame each of the three couples as they are ten years after their weddings. Compare your versions with other people's and discuss the differences. Then write an essay on 'Lasting love and shaky love in *A Midsummer Night's Dream*'.

Themes: love (12)

Events in the wood
In groups of seven, take on the roles of Bottom, Egeus, the four lovers and a news reporter for the *Athens Independent*. Conduct improvised interviews, probing into what really happened in the wood. Then create a newspaper front page, with individuals and pairs in the group taking responsibility for each of the following articles:
• the lovers' experiences
• Bottom's experiences
• Egeus's comments ('A worried father')
• the sudden improvement in the weather (look back at 2.1.88–117)
• the coming triple wedding.

Use quotations from the interviews and refer back to the script for other details.

5.1 Theseus's palace in Athens

It is the wedding night. Theseus and Hippolyta discuss the lovers' strange story and the power of the imagination.

Activities

Character review: Theseus and Hippolyta (1)

'More strange than true'

What is Theseus's opinion of the lovers' account of their experiences? What view does Hippolyta take? Why do you think Shakespeare gives Theseus and Hippolyta different opinions here?

Themes: theatrical illusion (2)

'The poet's eye …'

People have often remarked that Theseus's account of how a poet works (lines 12–17) can be applied to Shakespeare himself. For each of Theseus's comments listed below, explain how each comment can apply to what Shakespeare has done in *A Midsummer Night's Dream*:

(a) 'The poet's eye, in a fine frenzy rolling'
(b) 'Doth glance from heaven to earth, from earth to heaven'
(c) 'And, as imagination bodies forth
The forms of things unknown, the poet's pen
Turns them to shapes,'
(d)   'and gives to airy nothing
A local habitation and a name.'

3 **antique** (1) old; (2) ridiculous
   fairy toys silly fairytales

4 **seething** frantically active

5 **shaping fantasies** fertile imaginations

5–6 **apprehend … comprehend** their imaginations can grasp things which their intelligence cannot understand rationally

8 **Are of … compact** (1) are made up entirely of the imagination; (2) share the same kinds of imagination

11 **sees Helen's … Egypt** thinks an ugly woman is beautiful

12 **fine frenzy** noble burst of inspiration

14 **bodies forth** gives birth to; gives a physical shape to

16 **airy nothing** pure imagination

17 **a local habitation** a place in which to live

19 **apprehend** experience

20 **comprehends** includes

24 **transfigured so together** changed in the same way and at the same time

25–27 **more witnesseth … admirable** testifies that there was more going on than merely pictures created by the imagination, and builds up into a consistent story – at the same time, outside our normal experience and to be wondered at

31 **board** food-table

Act 5

Scene 1

Athens.

Enter THESEUS, HIPPOLYTA, PHILOSTRATE *and* Attendants.

HIPPOLYTA   'T is strange, my Theseus, that these lovers speak of.

THESEUS   More strange than true. I never may believe
             These antique fables nor these fairy toys.
             Lovers and madmen have such seething brains,
             Such shaping fantasies, that apprehend   5
             More than cool reason ever comprehends.
             The lunatic, the lover, and the poet
             Are of imagination all compact.
             One sees more devils than vast hell can hold;
             That is the madman. The lover, all as frantic, 10
             Sees Helen's beauty in a brow of Egypt.
             The poet's eye, in a fine frenzy rolling,
             Doth glance from heaven to earth, from earth to
                 heaven,
             And as imagination bodies forth
             The forms of things unknown, the poet's pen   15
             Turns them to shapes, and gives to airy nothing
             A local habitation and a name.
             Such tricks hath strong imagination
             That, if it would but apprehend some joy,
             It comprehends some bringer of that joy.   20
             Or in the night, imagining some fear,
             How easy is a bush supposed a bear.

HIPPOLYTA   But all the story of the night told over,
             And all their minds transfigured so together,
             More witnesseth than fancy's images,   25
             And grows to something of great constancy;
             But howsoever, strange and admirable.

Enter LYSANDER, DEMETRIUS, HERMIA *and* HELENA.

THESEUS   Here come the lovers, full of joy and mirth:
             Joy, gentle friends, joy and fresh days of love
             Accompany your hearts!

LYSANDER   More than to us,   30
             Wait in your royal walks, your board, your bed!

5.1 Theseus's palace in Athens

Philostrate, master of the revels, gives Theseus a list of all the entertainments on offer. Theseus rejects the first three but is attracted by the idea of the mechanicals' play.

Activities

Actors' interpretations: 'We'll none of that'

How should the actor playing Theseus read out the list of entertainments (lines 44–60)? From what you know of Theseus, work out a suitable reaction to each item and then act out the speech.

Alex Jennings as Theseus reading the list of entertainments to other members of the cast (RSC 1994)

32 **masques** *courtly plays involving music*

34 **after-supper** *the final course of a banquet*

39 **abridgement** *entertainment to make the time pass more quickly*

40 **beguile** *deceive* (*pass the time without realising it*)

42 **brief** summary, short list

ripe ready to be performed

45 **eunuch** *castrated male who sang in an unbroken voice*

48 **tipsy Bacchanals** *women who tore Orpheus apart while they were drunkenly worshipping Bacchus (see page 170)*

50 **device** show

52 **Muses** *Each of the nine Muses in classical myth was responsible for a different branch of the arts.*

52–53 **'... mourning for ... beggary'** *Poets and playwrights in Shakespeare's time often complained that they were starving for lack of money.*

54 **keen** sharp, biting

55 **Not sorting ... ceremony** inappropriate for a wedding celebration

56 **tedious** boring, tiresome

60 **concord of this discord** the consistency within these contradictions

65 **fitted** suited to his part

THESEUS	Come now, what masques, what dances shall we have
	To wear away this long age of three hours
	Between our after-supper, and bed-time?
	Where is our usual manager of mirth? 35
	What revels are in hand? Is there no play
	To ease the anguish of a torturing hour?
	Call Philostrate.

PHILOSTRATE   Here, mighty Theseus.

THESEUS	Say, what abridgement have you for this evening?
	What masque? What music? How shall we beguile 40
	The lazy time, if not with some delight?

PHILOSTRATE There is a brief how many sports are ripe:
     Make choice of which your Highness will see first.

THESEUS   (*reads*)
     'The battle with the Centaurs, to be sung
     By an Athenian eunuch, to the harp'. 45
     We'll none of that. That have I told my love
     In glory of my kinsman Hercules.
     'The riot of the tipsy Bacchanals,
     Tearing the Thracian singer in their rage'.
     That is an old device, and it was played 50
     When I from Thebes came last a conqueror.
     'The thrice three Muses, mourning for the death
     Of Learning, late deceased in beggary'.
     That is some satire, keen and critical,
     Not sorting with a nuptial ceremony. 55
     'A tedious brief scene of young Pyramus
     And his love Thisby; very tragical mirth'.
     Merry and tragical? Tedious, and brief?
     That is, hot ice, and wondrous strange snow.
     How shall we find the concord of this discord? 60

PHILOSTRATE A play there is, my lord, some ten words long,
     Which is as brief as I have known a play;
     But by ten words, my lord, it is too long,
     Which makes it tedious; for in all the play
     There is not one word apt, one player fitted. 65

5.1 Theseus's palace in Athens

Philostrate explains that the mechanicals' play is laughably awful, but Theseus insists on seeing it, as the simple workmen have no doubt done their best.

Activities

Character review: Philostrate

How does he react?

In some productions a joke is made of the fact that the 'manager of mirth' (line 35) is extremely serious and gloomy.

1. In pairs, practise reading Philostrate's conversation with Theseus in different ways, with Philostrate sounding (for example) extremely amused or snobbish and superior. How far does he go in trying to discourage Theseus from seeing the mechanicals' play?

2. Improvise an off-stage conversation between Philostrate and his assistant, in which he comments on Theseus's choice and praises the rejected performances (lines 44–53).

Character review: Theseus and Hippolyta (2)

Another disagreement

Once more they disagree (and not for the last time – see lines 205–211).

- Why is Hippolyta reluctant to see 'Pyramus and Thisby'?
- What point is Theseus making about himself and 'great clerks' (lines 93–105)?
- What does Theseus mean by 'Our sport ... merit' (lines 90–92)?

70 **passion** emotion

71 **What** what kind of men

74 **toiled their unbreathed memories** taxed their little-used powers of memory (*in learning their lines*)

75 **against your nuptial** in preparation for your wedding

79 **find sport in their intents** get a laugh out of their attempts

80 **stretched and ... pain** they have stretched their abilities to the limit and have tormented themselves in learning the lines

82 **amiss** wrong

83 **tender** offer

85–86 **I love not ... perishing** I hate to see less able (*or perhaps:* lower-class) people pushed beyond their capabilities (**wretchedness o'ercharged**) and people failing when they attempt to offer loyal service

90 **our sport ... mistake** Our pleasure will be to accept what they offer, even if they get it wrong

91–92 **noble respect ... merit** the gracious way of looking at it, is to value their intentions, rather than what they actually achieve

93 **clerks** scholars

94 **premeditated** pre-planned

96 **make periods** pause

97 **practised accent** rehearsed delivery

And tragical, my noble lord, it is;
For Pyramus therein doth kill himself.
Which when I saw rehearsed, I must confess,
Made mine eyes water; but more merry tears,
The passion of loud laughter never shed.   70

THESEUS   What are they that do play it?

PHILOSTRATE Hard-handed men, that work in Athens here,
Which never laboured in their minds till now;
And now have toiled their unbreathed memories
With this same play, against your nuptial.   75

THESEUS   And we will hear it.

PHILOSTRATE   No, my noble lord,
It is not for you. I have heard it over,
And it is nothing, nothing in the world;
Unless you can find sport in their intents,
Extremely stretched and conned with cruel pain,   80
To do you service.

THESEUS   I will hear that play.
For never any thing can be amiss
When simpleness and duty tender it.
Go, bring them in; and take your places, ladies.

                                        Exit PHILOSTRATE.

HIPPOLYTA   I love not to see wretchedness o'ercharged,   85
And duty in his service perishing.

THESEUS   Why, gentle sweet, you shall see no such thing.

HIPPOLYTA   He says they can do nothing in this kind.

THESEUS   The kinder we, to give them thanks for nothing.
Our sport shall be take what they mistake;   90
And what poor duty cannot do, noble respect
Takes it in might, not merit.
Where I have come, great clerks have purposéd
To greet me with premeditated welcomes;
Where I have seen them shiver and look pale,   95
Make periods in the midst of sentences,
Throttle their practised accent in their fears,

5.1 Theseus's palace in Athens

The play begins. Peter Quince stumbles through his prologue, and then the others enter in costume: Bottom as Pyramus, Flute as Thisby, Snout as Wall, Starveling as Moonshine and Snug as Lion.

Activities

Shakespeare's language: '... the Prologue is addressed'

Re-read Peter Quince's prologue (lines 108–117).

1. Act it out, emphasising all the mistaken meanings which arise from his faulty punctuation.
2. Here is a possible version of the first ten lines as Quince might have intended them. What are the main messages he actually wants to get across?

If we offend, it is with our good will
That you should think we come – not
   to offend –
But with good will to show our simple
   skill:
That is the true beginning of our end.
Consider then, we come (but *in
   despite*
We do not come) as minding to
   content you.
Our true intent is all for your delight.
We are not here that you should here
   repent you.
The actors are at hand: and by their
   show,
You shall know all that you are like to
   know.

101 **modesty** feelings of deference and duty

103 **audacious eloquence** over-confident smooth-talking

104 **simplicity** sincerity

105 **in least ... capacity** say most in few words, in my opinion

106 **addressed** ready to begin

112 **in despite** in order to irritate you

113 **as minding** with the intention

118 **stand upon points** (1) take notice of punctuation; (2) bother about insignificant details

119 **rid** (1) ridden; (2) got rid of

   rough unbroken

120 **stop** (1) full stop; (2) the sudden halt of a horse

123 **in government** under control

125 **impaired** broken

And in conclusion, dumbly have broke off,
Not paying me a welcome. Trust me, sweet,
Out of this silence yet I picked a welcome;   100
And in the modesty of fearful duty
I read as much as from the rattling tongue
Of saucy and audacious eloquence.
Love, therefore, and tongue-tied simplicity,
In least speak most, to my capacity.   105

Re-enter PHILOSTRATE.

PHILOSTRATE So please your Grace, the Prologue is addressed.

THESEUS Let him approach.

Trumpets sound. Enter QUINCE *as the* PROLOGUE.

QUINCE (*as* PROLOGUE)
If we offend, it is with our good will.
That you should think, we come not to offend,
But with good will. To show our simple skill,   110
That is the true beginning of our end.
Consider then, we come but in despite.
We do not come, as minding to content you,
Our true intent is. All for your delight,
We are not here. That you should here repent you,   115
The actors are at hand: and by their show,
You shall know all that you are like to know.

THESEUS This fellow doth not stand upon points.

LYSANDER He hath rid his prologue like a rough colt: he
knows not the stop. A good moral, my lord: it is   120
not enough to speak, but to speak true.

HIPPOLYTA Indeed he hath played on his prologue like a child
on a recorder, a sound but not in government.

THESEUS His speech was like a tangled chain: nothing
impaired, but all disordered. Who is next?   125

A trumpet sounds. Enter PYRAMUS (BOTTOM), THISBE (FLUTE), WALL
(SNOUT), MOONSHINE (STARVELING), *and* LION (SNUG), *who stand in
line while* QUINCE *speaks as* PROLOGUE.

5.1 Theseus's palace in Athens

As Prologue, Peter Quince introduces each character and gives an outline of the story. All the actors leave the stage except Snout, who explains that he represents the wall which kept the lovers apart, but which had a chink through which they could whisper.

Activities

Actors' interpretations: blocking the scene

This is a difficult scene to stage because the mechanicals have to perform as though facing two audiences: the court and us, the theatre audience. Which way should they face? Where should the court be sitting?

Copy the diagram of Shakespeare's stage on page 168 and mark in:
- where the court characters are sitting or standing
- where the mechanicals will perform 'Pyramus and Thisby'.

In groups of six, compare your different diagrams. Pick one of them and act out the 'dumb show' (lines 126–150) as Quince narrates it. Then try someone else's ideas and decide which staging works best.

131 **sunder** keep apart

134 **with lantern ...** *see 3.1.58–60*

136 **did think no scorn** didn't think it beneath them

138 **hight** is called (*an old-fashioned 'poetic' word*)

141 **fall** drop

143 **Anon** immediately

tall brave

146 **broached** pierced

150 **At large discourse** explain at length

153 **interlude** short play

156 **crannied** with a narrow opening

QUINCE   (*as* PROLOGUE)
Gentles, perchance you wonder at this show;
But wonder on, till truth make all things plain.
This man is Pyramus, if you would know;
This beauteous lady Thisby is certain.
This man with lime and rough-cast doth present   130
Wall, that vile Wall, which did these lovers sunder:
And through Wall's chink, poor souls, they are
    content
To whisper: at the which, let no man wonder.
This man, with lantern, dog, and bush of thorn,
Presenteth Moonshine; for, if you will know,   135
By moonshine did these lovers think no scorn
To meet at Ninus' tomb, there, there to woo.
This grisly beast, which Lion hight by name,
The trusty Thisby, coming first by night,
Did scare away, or rather did affright: 140
And as she fled, her mantle she did fall;
Which Lion vile with bloody mouth did stain.
Anon comes Pyramus, sweet youth and tall,
And finds his trusty Thisby's mantle slain;
Whereat with blade, with bloody blameful blade,   145
He bravely broached his boiling bloody breast,
And Thisby, tarrying in mulberry shade,
His dagger drew, and died. For all the rest,
Let Lion, Moonshine, Wall, and Lovers twain,
At large discourse, while here they do remain.   150

Exeunt all the players *but* SNOUT (WALL).

THESEUS   I wonder if the lion be to speak.

DEMETRIUS   No wonder, my lord: one lion may, when many
    asses do.

SNOUT   (*as* WALL)
In this same interlude it doth befall
That I, one Snout by name, present a wall:
And such a wall, as I would have you think,   155
That had in it a crannied hole or chink,
Through which the lovers, Pyramus and Thisby,
Did whisper often, very secretly.
This loam, this rough-cast, and this stone doth
    show

5.1 Theseus's palace in Athens

Pyramus (Bottom) approaches the wall and peeps through the chink. Unable to see Thisby, he curses the wall and, after Bottom has explained to his court audience what is about to happen, Thisby (Flute) approaches.

Activities

Actors' interpretations: performing the wall

1. Re-read Bottom's suggestions (3.1.66–70) and then draw an annotated sketch of your ideal 'Pyramus and Thisby' wall.

2. In pairs perform Bottom's address to the wall (lines 166–177).
   - How should he deliver the lines? (Over-the-top or more restrained?)
   - How should Snout react to all the 'sweet and lovelies'?
   - How does Snout hold up his fingers on line 173? (In one production, Snout was unwilling to play wall and gave Bottom a V-sign. Bottom's reply 'Thanks, courteous wall' was sarcastic.)
   - What actions does Pyramus perform when looking through the chink and cursing the wall? How does the wall react in each case?

161 **right and sinister** right and left (*i.e. horizontal*)

164 **wittiest partition** (1) cleverest wall; (2) best-written section of a speech

166 **hue** colour

168 **alack** *an expression of misery like 'alas!'*

173 **eyne** eyes

178 **sensible** able to feel

curse again curse back

181 **all pat** happen exactly

	That I am that same Wall; the truth is so.	160
	And this the cranny is, right and sinister,	
	Through which the fearful lovers are to whisper.	

THESEUS   Would you desire lime and hair to speak better?

DEMETRIUS   It is the wittiest partition that ever I heard
                     discourse, my lord.

THESEUS   Pyramus draws near the Wall; silence.   165

Enter BOTTOM *as* PYRAMUS.

BOTTOM   (*as* PYRAMUS)
                     O grim-looked night, O night with hue so black!
                     O night, which ever art when day is not!
                     O night, O night; alack, alack, alack,
                     I fear my Thisby's promise is forgot.
                     And thou O wall, O sweet, O lovely wall,   170
                     That stand'st between her father's ground and
                           mine,
                     Thou wall, O wall, O sweet and lovely wall,
                     Show me thy chink, to blink through with mine
                           eyne.

SNOUT *holds up his fingers.*

                     Thanks, courteous wall: Jove shield thee well for
                           this!
                     But what see I? No Thisby do I see.   175
                     O wicked wall, through whom I see no bliss,
                     Cursed be thy stones for thus deceiving me!

THESEUS   The wall, methinks, being sensible, should curse
                     again.

BOTTOM   No, in truth sir, he should not. 'Deceiving me' is
                     Thisby's cue; she is to enter now, and I am to spy   180
                     her through the wall. You shall see it will fall pat
                     as I told you: yonder she comes.

Enter FLUTE (*as* THISBE).

FLUTE   (*as* THISBE)
                     O wall, full often hast thou heard my moans,

5.1 Theseus's palace in Athens

Pyramus and Thisby talk through the chink. They declare their everlasting love for one another, agree to meet at 'Ninny's' tomb and depart. Wall politely takes his leave and exits after them.

Activities

Actors' interpretations: acting through the wall

Pyramus and Thisby's exchange through the wall (lines 183–199) can be one of the highlights of the mechanicals' play.

1. What does the wall do while the lovers are wooing?
2. When Shakespeare uses words with sexual double meanings we talk about 'bawdy innuendo'. How might the actors use 'stones' (which could mean 'testicles') and 'hole' for comic effect here? Are Bottom or Flute (or Snout!) aware of the double meanings, for example?
3. What special effect can be gained through the very short speeches?
4. Bearing in mind the decisions you have made about 1, 2 and 3, try performing the exchange in a variety of different ways (such as very fast, for example, or highly romantically). Which works best?

185 **stones** *This can also mean 'testicles'.*

186 **hair** *to help bind the plaster*

191 **thy lover's grace** *your gracious lover*

192 **Limander** *Bottom's version of Leander, a mythical hero who swam the Hellespont to visit his lover, Hero*

193 **Helen** *Flute's unfortunate mistake for Hero (Helen of Troy was not faithful – see page 171.)*

the Fates *In classical mythology, the three Fates determined a person's life-span (see page 170).*

194 **Shafalus ... Procrus** *further mispronunciations (Cephalus remained faithful to his wife Procris when he was abducted by Aurora, goddess of dawn.)*

199 **'Tide life ... death** *come life, come death*

For parting my fair Pyramus and me.
My cherry lips have often kissed thy stones;   185
Thy stones, with lime and hair knit up in thee.

BOTTOM   (*as* PYRAMUS)
I see a voice; now will I to the chink,
To spy an I can hear my Thisby's face.
Thisby!

FLUTE   (*as* THISBE)
My love! thou art my love, I think.   190

BOTTOM   (*as* PYRAMUS)
Think what thou wilt, I am thy lover's grace,
And like Limander am I trusty still.

FLUTE   (*as* THISBE)
And I like Helen, till the Fates me kill.

BOTTOM   (*as* PYRAMUS)
Not Shafalus to Procrus was so true.

FLUTE   (as THISBE)
As Shafalus to Procrus, I to you.   195

BOTTOM   (*as* PYRAMUS)
O kiss me through the hole of this vile wall.

FLUTE   (*as* THISBE)
I kiss the wall's hole, not your lips at all.

BOTTOM   (*as* PYRAMUS)
Wilt thou at Ninny's tomb meet me straightway?

FLUTE   (*as* THISBE)
'Tide life, 'tide death, I come without delay.

Exeunt BOTTOM *and* FLUTE.

SNOUT   (*as* WALL)
Thus have I, Wall, my part dischargéd so;   200
And being done, thus Wall away doth go.

Exit.

5.1 Theseus's palace in Athens

The court audience exchange comments on the performance and then Snug enters. He reassures them that he is not really a lion, but Snug the joiner.

Activities

Themes: theatrical illusion (3)

Yet another disagreement
This final disagreement between Theseus and Hippolyta (lines 204–209) is over the power of the imagination.

- What does Theseus mean by 'shadows' (line 207)?
- How important is imagination for (a) actors and (b) audiences?
- Where is the power of the imagination particularly important for an audience watching *A Midsummer Night's Dream*?

Janet McTeer as Hippolyta and Richard Easton as Theseus (RSC 1986)

---

202   **mural** wall

204–205   **when walls ... warning** *an allusion to the proverb 'walls have ears'*

207   **in this kind** of this type of person (*i.e. actors*)

  shadows representations of the real thing

208   **amend** improve

217–218   It's only as Snug playing a part that I am a fierce (**fell**) lion; and in no other way am I a lion or a lion's mother (**dam**)

219   **in strife** aggressively

223–224   **fox ... goose** *The lion was famous in fables for its bravery and kingly qualities, the fox for its cunning and the goose for its cowardice and stupidity.*

  discretion self-preservation

THESEUS	Now is the mural down between the two neighbours.

DEMETRIUS   No remedy, my lord, when walls are so wilful, to   205
hear without warning.

HIPPOLYTA   This is the silliest stuff that ever I heard.

THESEUS   The best in this kind are but shadows, and the
worst are no worse, if imagination amend them.

HIPPOLYTA   It must be your imagination then, and not theirs.

THESEUS   If we imagine no worse of them than they of   210
themselves, they may pass for excellent men. Here
come two noble beasts in, a man and a lion.

Enter SNUG *as* LION *and* STARVELING *as* MOONSHINE.

SNUG   (*as* LION)
You, ladies, you, whose gentle hearts do fear
The smallest monstrous mouse that creeps on
floor,
May now, perchance, both quake and tremble
here   215
When Lion rough in wildest rage doth roar.
Then know that I, one Snug the joiner, am
A lion fell, nor else no lion's dam:
For if I should as Lion come in strife
Into this place, 't were pity on my life.   220

THESEUS   A very gentle beast, and of a good conscience.

DEMETRIUS   The very best at a beast, my lord, that e'er I saw.

LYSANDER   This Lion is a very fox for his valour.

THESEUS   True, and a goose for his discretion.

DEMETRIUS   Not so, my lord; for his valour cannot carry his   225
discretion, and the fox carries the goose.

THESEUS   His discretion, I am sure, cannot carry his valour;
for the goose carries not the fox. It is well; leave it
to his discretion, and let us listen to the Moon.

5.1 Theseus's palace in Athens

When Starveling tries to explain his role as Moonshine, he is constantly interrupted. Then Flute arrives as Thisby and Snug utters a roar.

Activities

Actors' interpretations: 'The lanthorn doth ...'

A In groups of five, act out Starveling's attempts to deliver his speech (lines 230–253). How frustrated and angry should he become?

B In many productions the interruptions to Starveling's speech come across to the audience as extremely rude and unfair. Starveling is sometimes particularly hurt by Hippolyta's comment (lines 241–242). Act out lines 230–253 and talk about the meaning of the interruptions. Do you think Starveling is over-sensitive to be thrown off-course like this? Or do these interruptions actually show Theseus, Hippolyta and Demetrius in a very poor light?

C Write director's notes to this scene for a production which takes a marxist interpretation and concentrates on showing how the nobles exert their power over the workers. Which other parts of the play might be used to bring out a marxist interpretation? (Think about some of the relationships, such as Egeus and Hermia or Oberon and Puck, or Oberon and Titania.)

230 **lanthorn** lantern (*pronounced lant-horn, to allow Demetrius's pun – line 231*)

231 **horns on his head** *Men whose wives were unfaithful were called cuckolds; it was said that they grew horns.*

232 **no crescent** *The 'horns' of the moon are only visible when it is a crescent: they are the sharp points.*

239 **for** for fear of

240 **in snuff** (1) in need of snuffing (*trimming a candle*); (2) in a temper

243 **It appears ... discretion** *Perhaps Starveling is beginning to grow angry (lacking discretion).*

244 **in the wane** decreasing in size, 'on his way out'

245 **stay the time** wait patiently

247–250 **All I have ...** *In his exasperation, Starveling ditches the verse and resorts to prose.*

5.1

STARVELING	(*as* MOONSHINE)	
	This lanthorn doth the hornéd moon present.	230

DEMETRIUS   He should have worn the horns on his head.

THESEUS   He is no crescent and his horns are invisible,
within the circumference.

STARVELING   (*as* MOONSHINE)
This lanthorn doth the hornéd moon present:
Myself the Man i' th' Moon do seem to be.   235

THESEUS   This is the greatest error of all the rest; the man
should be put into the lantern. How is it else the
Man i' th' Moon?

DEMETRIUS   He dares not come there for the candle; for you
see, it is already in snuff.   240

HIPPOLYTA   I am a-weary of this Moon; would he would
change!

THESEUS   It appears, by his small light of discretion, that he
is in the wane: but yet, in courtesy, in all reason,
we must stay the time.   245

LYSANDER   Proceed, Moon.

STARVELING   (*as* MOONSHINE)
All that I have to say is to tell you that the
lanthorn is the Moon; I, the Man i' th' Moon; this
thorn-bush, my thorn-bush; and this dog, my
dog.   250

DEMETRIUS   Why, all these should be in the lantern: for all
these are in the Moon. But silence, here comes
Thisby.

Re-enter FLUTE (*as* THISBE).

FLUTE   (*as* THISBE)
This is old Ninny's tomb. Where is my love?

SNUG   (*as* LION) *roars*
Oh-h-h-!   255

5.1 Theseus's palace in Athens

Thisby runs off, frightened by the lion, and Pyramus enters. He is devastated to see her bloodstained cloak and, assuming she has been killed by the lion, utters a tragic speech.

Activities

Shakespeare's language: 'Sweet moon …'

What has Shakespeare done to make the language of Bottom's speech (lines 263–278) comic? Look, for example, at the sounds in lines 265, 267 and 278; the rhythm of lines 267–272; the ending of line 272.

Character review: Bottom (7)

His delivery
Think about Bottom's personality as it has been revealed throughout the play. What does it tell you about the ways in which he might deliver this speech (lines 263–278)? Act it out as you think Bottom would perform it and then compare your version with other people's. (A word of warning: if you make it too 'over-the-top', it ceases to be funny.)

260 **Well moused** *The lion savaging the mantle presumably looked like a cat, 'worrying' a mouse.*

266 **take of truest Thisby sight** get a sight of faithful Thisby

269 **dole** grief

272 **duck** darling

275 **Furies** *In classical myth, the Furies were snake-haired women who punished the guilty (see page 170).*

277 **cut thread and thrum** destroy everything (**thrum:** *the tufted end of the 'warp', the lengthways yarns in weaving*); *He is calling upon the Fates (see line 193 and page 170) to destroy all the threads that they have woven.*

278 **Quail** overpower

quell destroy

279 **passion** (1) suffering; (2) emotional speech

281 **Beshrew** curse

282 **wherefore** why

frame create

283 **deflowered my dear** taken my darling's virginity (*he means 'devoured'!*)

5.1

THISBE *runs off.*

DEMETRIUS	Well roared, Lion.
THESEUS	Well run, Thisby.
HIPPOLYTA	Well shone, Moon.
	Truly, the Moon shines with a good grace.

SNUG *(as* LION*) tears* THISBE*'s mantle, and exit.*

THESEUS	Well moused, Lion.	260

Re-enter BOTTOM *(as* PYRAMUS*).*

DEMETRIUS	And then came Pyramus.
LYSANDER	And so the Lion vanished.

BOTTOM	(*as* PYRAMUS)	
	Sweet Moon, I thank thee for thy sunny beams;	
	I thank thee, Moon, for shining now so bright;	
	For by thy gracious, golden, glittering gleams,	265
	I trust to take of truest Thisby sight.	
	But stay! O spite!	
	But mark, poor knight,	
	What dreadful dole is here!	
	Eyes, do you see?	270
	How can it be?	
	O dainty duck! O dear!	
	Thy mantle good,	
	What, stained with blood?	
	Approach, ye Furies fell:	275
	O Fates! come, come:	
	Cut thread and thrum,	
	Quail, crush, conclude, and quell!	
THESEUS	This passion, and the death of a dear friend,	
	would go near to make a man look sad.	280
HIPPOLYTA	Beshrew my heart, but I pity the man.	
BOTTOM	(*as* PYRAMUS)	
	O wherefore, Nature, didst thou lions frame?	
	Since lion vile hath here deflowered my dear:	

5.1 Theseus's palace in Athens

Drawing his sword, Pyramus kills himself in his grief, and, after some more comments from the court audience, Flute enters as Thisby.

Activities

Actors' interpretations: Pyramus's grief

When Hippolyta hears the first part of Pyramus's speech, she says 'Beshrew my heart, but I pity the man' (line 281). Act out this second part (lines 282–297), first ridiculously and comically, then as seriously as you can. Try other versions which are a mixture of the two and decide which works best.

Then write director's notes to help the actor playing Bottom to decide how best to approach the Pyramus speeches.

Robert Gillespie as Starveling/Moonshine and Des Barrit as Bottom/Pyramus (RSC 1994)

285 **cheer** face

289 **pap** breast

298 **die** one of a pair of dice (*'dice' was originally the plural*)

ace *the single spot on the die's face*

299 **less than an ace** *because he is dead (less than one = nothing)*

302 **ass** a pun (*it sounds like 'ace'*)

306 **passion** *see line 279*

309 **mote** speck of dust

310–311 **a man ... bless us!** May God forgive us for describing this Pyramus and Thisby as a man and a woman! (**warrant:** preserve)

Which is – no, no, which was – the fairest Dame
That lived, that loved, that liked, that looked with
    cheer.   285
Come tears, confound:
Out sword, and wound
The pap of Pyramus:
Ay, that left pap,
Where heart doth hop;   290
Thus die I, thus, thus, thus.

Stabs himself.

Now am I dead,
Now am I fled,
My soul is in the sky,
Tongue, lose thy light,   295
Moon, take thy flight,

Exit STARVELING *as* MOONSHINE.

Now die, die, die, die, die.   (*'Dies'*)

DEMETRIUS   No die, but an ace for him; for he is but one.

LYSANDER   Less than an ace, man; for he is dead, he is
    nothing.   300

THESEUS   With the help of a surgeon he might yet recover,
    and prove an ass.

HIPPOLYTA   How chance Moonshine is gone before Thisby
    comes back, and finds her lover?

Re-enter FLUTE *(as* THISBE*).*

THESEUS   She will find him by starlight. Here she comes, and 305
    her passion ends the play.

HIPPOLYTA   Methinks she should not use a long one for such a
    Pyramus; I hope she will be brief.

DEMETRIUS   A mote will turn the balance, which Pyramus,
    which Thisby is the better; he for a man, God   310
    warrant us, she for a woman, God bless us.

LYSANDER   She hath spied him already with those sweet eyes.

5.1 Theseus's palace in Athens

As soon as Thisby realises that her beloved Pyramus is not asleep but dead, she takes his sword and kills herself. The play has ended and Bottom leaps up to offer an epilogue or a dance.

Activities

Shakespeare's language: the unused epilogue

Write the epilogue that Peter Quince has prepared, but which is never delivered (lines 340–344).

- Think first about the kind of thing Quince might want to say in an epilogue. It will help to look at Shakespeare's own epilogue for *Henry V* and Puck's concluding speech in this play. Often the character speaking the epilogue will:
  - ask the audience's forgiveness for any deficiencies in the play
  - say something about the next play which continues the story (has Quince got one in mind?); ask for some applause.
- You could use the verse form of his prologue (lines 108–117) or something nearer to the rhythm and rhyme of Bottom's speech (lines 263–278).

313 **videlicet** namely; in other words (*Latin; often abbreviated to viz.*)

326 **Sisters Three** the Fates (*see line 192*)

330 **shore** shorn, cut (*one of the Fates, Atropos, cut off each person's thread of life – line 331*)

334 **imbrue** stab (*possibly also:* stain with blood)

342 **epilogue** *a speech delivered at the end of a play (like Puck's final words in this play, or the Chorus's in* Henry V)

Bergomask *a clod-hopping country dance (named after the town of Bergamo in Italy)*

DEMETRIUS   And she moans, *videlicet:*

FLUTE   (*as* THISBE)
Asleep, my love?
What, dead, my dove?   315
O Pyramus, arise!
Speak, speak. Quite dumb?
Dead, dead? A tomb
Must cover thy sweet eyes.
These lily lips,   320
This cherry nose,
These yellow cowslip cheeks,
Are gone, are gone:
Lovers, make moan:
His eyes were green as leeks.   325
O Sisters Three,
Come, come to me,
With hands as pale as milk;
Lay them in gore,
Since you have shore   330
With shears his thread of silk.
Tongue, not a word:
Come, trusty sword:
Come blade, my breast imbrue:

Stabs herself.

And farewell, friends;   335
Thus Thisby ends;
Adieu, adieu, adieu. (*'Dies'*)

THESUES   Moonshine and Lion are left to bury the dead.

DEMETRIUS   Ay, and Wall too.

BOTTOM   (*getting up*)
No, I assure you, the wall is down that parted   340
their fathers. Will it please you to see the
epilogue, or to hear a Bergomask dance between
two of our company?

THESEUS   No epilogue, I pray you; for your play needs no
excuse. Never excuse; for when the players are all   345
dead there need none to be blamed. Marry, if he

5.1 Theseus's palace in Athens

Theseus explains why their play does not need an epilogue and the mechanicals dance instead. As the bell tolls midnight, the lovers go off to bed and Puck appears, followed by Oberon, Titania and the fairies.

Activities

Actors' interpretatons: performing the dance

In groups of six, find some appropriate music (or play it yourself) and work out a dance that might be suitable for the mechanicals' heavy-footed Bergomask.

Shakespeare's language: 'Now the hungry lion roars ...'

Imagine you were filming the play and had decided to have Puck's speech (lines 360–379) heard in 'voice-over' while the pictures he describes were actually seen. Draw a series of story-board frames to show what the sequence might look like.

David Troughton as Bottom and other members of the cast performing the Bergomask (RSC 1989)

350 **discharged** performed

352 **told** (1) counted out loud; (2) tolled

355 **overwatched** stayed up too long

356 **palpable gross** obviously crude

hath well ... night has successfully helped the slow hours of night to pass quickly

358 **this solemnity** these ceremonies

361 **behowls** howls at

362 **heavy** weary

363 **fordone** exhausted

364 **wasted brands** burnt-out logs

366–367 **Puts the wretch ... shroud** causes people lying awake miserably to think about death (*the dead were buried in shroud*s)

370 **Every one ... sprite** each grave releases its ghost

373 **triple Hecate's team** *The chariot of the goddess Hecate, drawn by dragons ('triple' because she was Luna (or Cynthia or Phoebe) in heaven, Diana (or Artemis) on earth and Proserpina or Hecate in the underworld).*

376 **frolic** high-spirited

378 **with broom** *Robin Goodfellow was believed to keep the house clean.*

that writ it had played Pyramus, and hanged
himself in Thisby's garter, it would have been a
fine tragedy: and so it is truly, and very notably
discharged. But come, your Bergomask: let your   350
epilogue alone.

A Bergomask dance.

The iron tongue of midnight hath told twelve.
Lovers, to bed; 't is almost fairy time.
I fear we shall out-sleep the coming morn
As much as we this night have overwatched.   355
This palpable gross play hath well beguiled
The heavy gait of night. Sweet friends, to bed.
A fortnight hold we this solemnity,
In nightly revels and new jollity.

Exeunt all.

Enter PUCK with a broom.

PUCK   Now the hungry lion roars,   360
And the wolf behowls the moon;
Whilst the heavy ploughman snores,
All with weary task fordone.
Now the wasted brands do glow,
Whilst the screech-owl, screeching loud,   365
Puts the wretch that lies in woe
In remembrance of a shroud.
Now it is the time of night
That the graves, all gaping wide,
Every one lets forth his sprite,   370
In the church-way paths to glide.
And we fairies, that do run
By the triple Hecate's team
From the presence of the sun,
Following darkness like a dream,   375
Now are frolic; not a mouse
Shall disturb this hallowed house.
I am sent with broom before,
To sweep the dust behind the door.

*Enter OBERON and TITANIA, the King and Queen of Fairies, with their train,
bearing lighted candles.*

5.1 Theseus's palace in Athens

Oberon and Titania tell their fairies to bless the three couples and the children who will be born to them. As they move off through the house, Puck is left behind.

Activities

Themes: order and disorder (3)

The ending

At the end of a Shakespeare comedy, directors will often wish to underline the sense of harmony and concord which accompanies the resolution of problems and the marriages of the lovers.

1. Look at the script and note down how this sense of harmony can be conveyed through:
   - movement (such as the dance)
   - visual effects (through lighting, for example, or the use of torches and glitter)
   - sound effects and music
   - the use of the language itself (rhythm, rhyme, choice of words).
2. Think about your own interpretation of the play. Is there any argument for an ending which questions the apparent harmony and suggests that disorder might be lurking beneath the surface? How would you convey that interpretation?

386 **rehearse ... by rote** repeat from memory

398–399 **the blots ... stand** their children (**issue**) will not bear any physical blemishes

401 **prodigious** ominous, regarded as an ill-omen

402 **in nativity** at birth

404 **consecrate** blessed, consecrated

405 **take his gait** go on his way

406 **several chamber** individual bedroom

412 **shadows** (1) fairies; (2) actors

OBERON	Through the house give glimmering light,	380
	By the dead and drowsy fire;	
	Every elf and fairy sprite	
	Hop as light as bird from brier;	
	And this ditty after me	
	Sing, and dance it trippingly.	385
TITANIA	First rehearse your song by rote,	
	To each word a warbling note.	
	Hand in hand, with fairy grace,	
	Will we sing and bless this place.	

OBERON leads, and the Fairies sing and dance.

OBERON	Now until the break of day,	390
	Through this house each fairy stray.	
	To the best bride-bed will we,	
	Which by us shall blessèd be;	
	And the issue there create	
	Ever shall be fortunate.	395
	So shall all the couples three	
	Ever true in loving be;	
	And the blots of Nature's hand	
	Shall not in their issue stand.	
	Never mole, hare-lip, nor scar,	400
	Nor mark prodigious, such as are	
	Despisèd in nativity,	
	Shall upon their children be.	
	With this field-dew consecrate,	
	Every fairy take his gait,	405
	And each several chamber bless,	
	Through this palace, with sweet peace;	
	And the owner of it blest	
	Ever shall in safety rest.	
	Trip away, make no stay;	410
	Meet me all by break of day.	

Exeunt, OBERON and TITANIA behind, the Fairies through the house. PUCK stays.

PUCK	If we shadows have offended,	
	Think but this, and all is mended,	
	That you have but slumbered here,	
	While these visions did appear.	415
	And this weak and idle theme,	

5.1 Theseus's palace in Athens

Puck asks us, the audience, to forgive the actors for any shortcomings and to give them some applause.

Activities

Themes: theatrical illusion (4)

'If we shadows have offended …'
Puck's speech is a kind of epilogue (see the activity on page 142). He seems to be making three connected points:
1. we are actors, and what you have seen is not 'real'
2. our play was not perfect but we will improve …
3. … if you forgive us and show your appreciation.

Look through the speech to see how these points are conveyed through the following groups of words:
- (point 1) shadows, slumbered, visions, dream
- (point 2) weak and idle theme, we will mend, make amends, restore amends
- (point 3) think but this, do not reprehend, If you pardon, Give me your hands

---

416–418 **And this … reprehend** (*To understand this, it is best to start with line 418:*) and, ladies and gentleman, do not find fault with (**reprehend**) this weak and trivial story (**idle theme**) which offers you nothing more than a dream

419 **mend** do it better next time

421 **If we … luck** if we're lucky (though we don't deserve it)

422 **serpent's tongue** hissing from the audience

423 **ere** before

426 **Give me your hands** (1) in shaking hands as friends; (2) by applauding

427 **restore amends** make amends (put things right) in return

No more yielding but a dream,
Gentles, do not reprehend:
If you pardon, we will mend.
And, as I am an honest Puck,   420
If we have unearnéd luck
Now to scape the serpent's tongue,
We will make amends ere long,
Else the Puck a liar call.
So, good night unto you all.   425
Give me your hands, if we be friends,
And Robin shall restore amends.

Exit.

Exam practice

Actors' interpretations: directing 'Pyramus and Thisby'

Imagine you are going to direct 'Pyramus and Thisby' for your year group. Explain how you want the actor playing Flute to perform as Thisby and how to make his appearance as funny as possible.

Before you begin to write, you think about:
- what you would tell the student playing Flute about how to perform Thisby
- which moments in Thisby's appearances can be particularly funny
- what he should do to help the audience to enjoy the scene.

Actors' interpretations: performing 'Pyramus and Thisby'

A In groups, talk about the parts of 'Pyramus and Thisby' which you found funniest.

B Rehearse a class performance of 'Pyramus and Thisby' (5.1.108–348). Collect together any costumes and props you need (be original and practical in your decisions) and rehearse seriously. It will be most effective if the actors can learn their lines, but characters such as Theseus and the court audience could have theirs written on 'programmes' if necessary.

C Write Theseus's thank-you letter to Peter Quince and the mechanicals. Try to be honest in your comments on their efforts while at the same time saying nothing which could upset them. (You might decide whether it would be appropriate to apologise for the interruptions during Starveling's speech.)

Character review: Peter Quince (2)

After the play
1. Conduct a final interview with Peter Quince, asking him how the performance went. (He might proudly read out comments from the Duke's letter – see the previous activity.) Then write an article for the *Athens Independent* in which you quote Quince and also include some comments from Bottom and the others.
2. Write Quince's letter to any of the mechanicals, praising their performance and selecting highlights to comment on. Write to more than one mechanical to show how differently Quince might deal with each letter.

Themes: order and disorder (4)

A different interpretation
Look back at the activity on page 146 about the sense of harmony and concord which accompanies the resolution of problems and the marriages of the lovers.

Think about your own interpretation of the play. Is there any argument for an ending which questions the apparent harmony and suggests that disorder might be lurking beneath the surface? How might you convey that interpretation through:
(a) movement?
(b) visual effects such as lighting?
(c) sound effects and music?
(d) the use of the language itself (giving certain words unexpected emphasis, for example)?

Which kind of ending would you prefer for this play – one which reinforces the sense of order and harmony or questions it?

Activities

Thinking about the play as a whole . . .

Actor's interpretations

1 **(A)** *Filming the play*

Pick your favourite scene from the play and draw a sketch to show what a key moment might look like, adding notes to explain details of the characters' actions, expressions and gestures.

(B) *Staging scenes*

Pick two contrasting moments from the play (perhaps one near the beginning and one near the end) and, using the outline or plan on page 168, show how the moments might be staged to bring out the contrasts, writing annotations to explain your decisions. (You might, for example, choose two of the meetings between Oberon and Titania: 2.1 and 4.1.)

(C) *Directing an extract*

Annotate a short scene or extract to show actors' movements, actions and reactions. Introduce it with a statement about the particular interpretation that you are aiming for (such as a happy and harmonious ending to the play).

2 **(A)** *Casting the play*

If you had the chance to direct a performance of *A Midsummer Night's Dream* on stage, which actors and actresses would you cast in the following roles: Theseus, Hippolyta, Egeus, Philostrate, the four lovers, the six mechanicals, Puck, Oberon and Titania? Choose appropriate actors to play any six of these characters, explaining in each case why you think the particular performer would be right for the part.

(B) *A theatre programme*

Create a theatre programme for a production of *A Midsummer Night's Dream*. This might include:
- a cast list with the names of the actors
- some background material (for example, on fairies and magic – see page 169; or articles on the language or some of the major themes)
- details about Shakespeare and his plays (see pages 180–182).

C *A newspaper review*

Write your own review of *A Midsummer Night's Dream*, as a response to an actual theatre performance, or any one of the video versions that you have seen.

3 *Film versions*

There are some very old film versions of *A Midsummer Night's Dream*, but it is easiest to get hold of the video of the 1996 RSC/Channel 4 production and the recent film starring Kevin Kline as Bottom. It is also possible to acquire a video recording of the 1980 BBC TV production.

In groups, think up some ideas for a modern film adaptation of *A Midsummer Night's Dream* (possibly on the lines of Baz Luhrmann's 1997 film of *Romeo + Juliet*, with Claire Danes and Leonardo DiCaprio, set in modern-day 'Verona Beach'):
(a) Make decisions about actors to play the roles and locations for the different scenes of the story.
(b) Storyboard one of the key sequences and bring out the special qualities of your new interpretation.
(c) Discuss which features of the play (not only the story, but its themes and language) you would hope to bring out most successfully and which would be harder to get across.

4 **A** *An advertisement*

Create a poster or magazine advert for a new production of *A Midsummer Night's Dream*, featuring some of your favourite actors. First look at some examples in magazines, to see how images are used and what written material is included.

B *Video covers*

Discuss the two covers of video versions of *A Midsummer Night's Dream* shown on page 154.
• Which features of the story do they seem to be concentrating on? What 'image' is each one conveying? In what ways will the interpretations be different?
• Which characters have they decided to highlight?
• How have they arranged the images?
• What text have they used to 'sell' the product?

Create a video cover for your own screen production of the play (which might feature some of the performers chosen for activity A).

Activities

Warners, 1935

Glyndebourne, 1981

C *A display*

Put together a classroom display on *A Midsummer Night's Dream*, which would be interesting for a younger class approaching the play for the first time. Include:

- any drawings that you have done (staging designs, storyboards...)
- other background work (characters' letters and diary entries, the newspaper reports and page designs, the moon poster, the 'who-loves-whom?' chart...)
- anything else you can think of (a poster advertising the play; cartoons of images...)
- things that you have collected from productions (production postcards, programmes, reviews...).

You will need to write some introductory material, explaining what the play is about and how the various elements of the display tie in.

Character reviews

5   Character profiles

Many actors write systematic notes about the characters they are preparing to play. Draw up a CHARACTER PROFILE form on a word-processor and then fill it in for any characters you are working on. Headings might be:

NAME:

SOCIAL POSITION:

SUPER-OBJECTIVE: (the character's overriding aim, which drives them on, e.g. 'to get my play performed before the Duke and admired by the court')

LINE OF ACTION: (the practical things they must do to achieve that aim, e.g. 'rehearse and prepare')

OBSTACLES AGAINST IT: (e.g. 'my actors are not very experienced')

WHAT THE CHARACTER SAYS ABOUT HERSELF/HIMSELF:

WHAT OTHER CHARACTERS SAY ABOUT HER/HIM:

IMPRESSION ON FIRST APPEARANCE:

RELATIONSHIPS WITH OTHERS:

OTHER INFORMATION:

6 Character review: Nick Bottom

Ⓐ *Laughter and affection*

Look back through the play and pick one of the scenes in which Bottom appears. What does he do in that scene to make us (a) laugh at him; (b) like him?

Ⓑ *What he says*

Find six of these quotations of Bottom's and discuss what each one reveals about him:
- 'First, good Peter Quince, say what the play treats on: then read the names of the actors: and so grow to a point.'
- 'Masters, spread yourselves.'
- 'If I do it, let the audience look to their eyes: I will move storms…'
- 'I could play Ercles rarely…'
- '…let me play Thisby too'
- 'I will roar, that I will make the Duke say, "Let him roar again…"'
- 'Enough; hold or cut bowstrings.'
- 'There are things in this comedy of Pyramus and Thisby that will never please.'
- 'I have a device to make all well'
- '…to bring in, God shield us, a lion among ladies is a most dreadful thing…'
- 'Some man or other must present Wall'
- 'I see their knavery: this is to make an ass of me…'
- 'Methinks I have a great desire to a bottle of hay'
- 'I have had a most rare vision.'
- 'The eye of man hath not heard…'
- 'No, in truth, sir, he should not. "Deceiving me" is Thisby's cue…'

Write a short piece entitled 'Six features of Nick Bottom'.

Activities

C *An attractive character*

(a) Why is Bottom such a favourite of audiences? What is at the heart of his comedy? (Think about the suggestion that he is the classic comic character: a very ordinary person who puffs himself up with delusions that he is much grander and more talented than he really is.)

(b) Write an essay on the opportunities offered to an actor for humour in the role. Refer where possible to particular performances that you have seen and the class activities you have taken part in.

7 Character review: Puck

A *His importance*

How important is Puck in this story? Look back through the play and list all the things that he does which have an affect on the way people behave and which change the course of events.

B *His viewpoint*

Write Puck's own account of the hours following his meeting with the fairy (2.1) through to the wedding celebrations and the blessing of the house. Include:

- his feelings about Oberon
- his attitude towards the things Oberon asked him to do
- his reaction to all the different events, including his own mistakes
- his view of the way things turned out between Oberon and Titania.

Which happenings have given him particular pleasure?

C *Performing Puck*

How would Puck be presented in your production of the play? Richard McCabe played him as a mischievous schoolboy (RSC, 1989), Barry Lynch as a kind of clown (RSC, 1994); in some productions he has been a fierce wood spirit; and there is a long tradition of women playing the part. Compare the interpretations which are on video if you can and also talk about the other ways in which Puck might be presented.

8 Character review: Oberon, Titania and the fairies

A *The supernatural characters*

Look back through the play and draw a chart which represents the scenes in which the supernatural characters appear. What arguments do they have among themselves? What influence do they have on the behaviour of the mortals?

B *The world of the supernatural*

Draw up a poster which provides an illustrated explanation of the supernatural world of the play. Use photographs or your own artwork to represent moments from the play and explain features such as:

- the different kinds of supernatural beings encountered in the play
- the different powers they seem to possess
- the influence they have over the mortals.

Part of your poster might be devoted to an illustration of the different ways in which the supernatural characters can be represented in performance.

C *What they represent*

Many productions have taken the view that the supernatural beings represent some feature of the universe we inhabit. What is your view of the following interpretations?

The supernatural beings represent:

- disorder and lawlessness, in contrast to the mortals' ordered society, controlled by laws
- the inexplicable, in contrast to understandable daily phenomena
- natural forces, in contrast to civilisation
- emotion, in contrast to reason.

Another view is that the supernatural beings are agents for an accelerated version of human existence: in other words, the interference of Oberon and Puck, and their use of the magic love-juice simply speeds up what was going to happen anyway between the lovers.

Write an essay which evaluates each of these interpretations, and any others that you might have considered.

9   Character review: Hermia, Helena, Lysander and Demetrius

A *A horoscope*

Write the horoscope for one of the four lovers to cover the week in which midsummer night falls. What kinds of things might it say about:

- travel
- meeting people
- unusual happenings
- relationships with friends of the same sex
- love?

Activities

B *An autobiography*

Write a chapter from the autobiography of one of the four lovers, written some years later, which covers the events portrayed in the play. When you are writing as Hermia, say, remember that you can only be sure of the events that you think you experienced (but you can include accounts given to you by the other three). Is there anything that still puzzles you?

C *Distinguishing the characters*

How does Shakespeare distinguish between Helena and Hermia? Is there anything to distinguish Lysander from Demetrius? What is there which helps to individualise these characters (a) in Shakespeare's script; and (b) in performances that you have seen or thought about?

10 **Character review: Quince, Flute, Snout, Starveling, Snug, Theseus, Hippolyta, Egeus, Philostrate**

A *Quotations*

Pick one of these characters and select five quotations, like those in activity 6B, which represent the character's qualities. Then ask your partner to find the quotations and say what each one reveals about the character.

B *Acting the role*

What opportunities are there for actors playing these characters? Pick one character, look at the scenes in which he or she appears and describe what satisfaction or enjoyment exists in playing the part. (You could write this from the actor's point of view, using his or her 'voice'.)

C *Doubling*

(a) In many productions the part of Theseus is doubled with Oberon, Hippolyta with Titania and Philostrate with Puck. What opportunities does this offer for interesting interpretations? Why is this a useful arrangement in practical terms?

(b) Shakespeare's company went in for extensive doubling (a term that can include playing more than just *two* roles). Many modern companies do the same: wage bills are high and companies are accordingly small. Work out a system of doubling for a production of *A Midsummer Night's Dream* which will involve using the smallest number of actors possible. What interesting interpretations arise (when Quince doubles Peaseblossom, for example)? What are the most challenging practical difficulties (for the actor doubling Theseus and Oberon, for example)?

Thinking about the play as a whole …

Shakespeare's language

11 There are language activities on pages 2, 12, 16, 24, 42, 56, 88, 106, 112, 126, 138, 142, 144.

Ⓐ *A poster*

Re-read the activities on pages 24, 56 and 112 and create a poster for the classroom with the title 'The language of the mechanicals in *A Midsummer Night's Dream*'.

Ⓑ *Language effects*

Pick one of the following and write about its effects:

- Bottom's and Quince's malapropisms and confused senses (what does this add to the comedy?)
- the language of the magic spells (how does this help to build an atmosphere of mystery and magic?)
- the references to classical mythology (what contribution do they make to the idea that we are witnessing an ancient story with dream-like qualities?).

Ⓒ *Language variety*

Use the ideas from A and B to write about the variety in the language of *A Midsummer Night's Dream* and the different effects it achieves.

Themes

12 A theme is an important subject which seems to arise at several times in the play, showing in what the characters do and the language they use, so that we receive different perspectives on it. Themes in *A Midsummer Night's Dream* include the following (with activities in brackets):

- Love (pages 2, 4, 14, 25, 44, 52, 53, 64, 99, 108, 118, 119)
- Theatrical illusion (pages 58–60, 120, 134 and 148)
- Order and disorder (pages 32–34, 70, 146 and 150)
- Dreams (page 92).

1. Draw up a spider diagram which includes all the many references you can find to the theme of love in the play. Then create a collage which illustrates how the theme is developed and explored.
2. Look back at the activities on the theme of theatrical illusion and write about:
   - how the theme is developed and explored in the play;
   - what it adds to your overall interpretation of the play's meanings.

3. Look back at the activities on the theme of order and disorder. What kind of disorder was particularly disturbing to Shakespeare's audience, would you say? Think about:
- children opposing their parents (Act 1)
- disturbances in the natural world (pages 32–34)
- conflicts between rulers of kingdoms (pages 32–34)
- disturbances in the heavens affecting the earth (page 70).

Does the play suggest that there will always be disorder, or that there is a kind of natural order and harmony which will always be supreme in the end?

4. Write an account of the themes in *A Midsummer Night's Dream*, showing how the themes are developed and the key words recur, to contribute to the overall meanings of the play.

13 Re-read the activity on page 92 and think about the title of this play: what kind of 'dream' has been going on?

How many layers of 'dream' can be found in the play? Is the forest a dream-world, while Athens represents reality? Have we, the audience, been 'dreaming', as Puck suggests we have at the end? Have individual characters been dreaming (such as Bottom or Titania)? Has no one been dreaming at all? Are all plays 'dreams' anyway (think about the connection between dreams and the theme of theatrical illusion)?

Look back through the play and find all the references to dreams and visions. Then try to answer some of the questions raised above in an essay which explores the meaning behind the title of Shakespeare's play.

Plot review

14 Re-tell the story of the play as:

A *Acrostic*

a 'MIDSUMMER NIGHT' acrostic (in this case, a 14-line poem, the first line beginning with M, then I, then D… and so on)

B *Mini-saga*

a prose story of *exactly* fifty words, no more, no less

C *Sonnet*

similar to the one spoken by the Chorus at the end of *Henry V*, or an epilogue written in the same verse form as Puck's final speech.

Background to Shakespeare and *A Midsummer Night's Dream*

Do some research in an encyclopedia or CD-ROM to find out more about the background features highlighted in **bold**. There are also activities for additional research.

Shakespeare's England

Shakespeare lived during a period called the **Renaissance**: a time when extraordinary changes were taking place, especially in the fields of religion, politics, science, language and the arts. He wrote during the reigns of **Elizabeth I** and **James I**.

Religion and politics

- In the century following the **Reformation** in 1534, people in Shakespeare's England began to view the world and their own place in it very differently.
- Queen Elizabeth felt that she had to stand alone against a strongly Catholic Europe and maintain the **Protestant religion** in England established by her father Henry VIII.
- England had become a proud and independent nation, and a leading military and trading power, especially after the defeat of the **Spanish Armada** in 1588.
- People began to think about the relationship between themselves as individuals and the authority of the state, while not everybody any longer accepted the idea that queens or kings ruled by '**divine right**' (on God's authority).
- There were divisions in the Protestant church, with extremist groups such as the **Puritans** disapproving of much that they saw in society and the Church.
- James I succeeded Elizabeth in 1603. He was a Scot, interested in witchcraft, and a supporter of the theatre, who fought off the treasonous attempt of the **Gunpowder Plot** in 1605.
- People began to question the traditional beliefs in rank and social order – the ideas that some people should be considered superior simply because they were born into wealthy families; or that those in power should always be obeyed without question.

- As trade became increasingly important, it was not only the nobility who could become wealthy. People could move around the country more easily and a competitive **capitalist economy** developed.

Science and discovery

- Scientists began to question traditional authorities (the accepted ideas handed down from one generation to the next) and depended instead upon their own observation of the world, especially after the development of instruments such as the telescope. **Galileo** came into conflict with the Church for claiming that the Earth was not the centre of the universe.
- Explorers brought back new produce, such as spices, silks and gold, and created great excitement in the popular imagination for stories of distant lands and their peoples.

Language

- The more traditional scholars still regarded **Latin** as the only adequate language for scholarly discussion and writing (and liked it because it also prevented many 'uncultured' people from understanding philosophy, medicine, etc.).
- But a new interest in the **English language** came with England's growing importance and sense of identity.
- The Protestants favoured a personal relationship with God, which meant being able to read the Bible themselves (rather than letting priests interpret it for them). This led to the need for a good version in English and **The Authorised Version of the Bible** (the 'King James Bible') was published in 1611.
- **Grammar schools** sprang up after the Reformation which increased literacy (but mostly among males in the middle and upper classes, and mainly in London).
- The invention of the **printing press** in the 1450s had led to more people having access to information and new ideas – not just the scholars.
- The English language began to be standardised in this period (into **Standard English**), but it was still very flexible and there was less insistence on following rules than there is nowadays.
- There was an enormous expansion in **vocabulary**, which affected every area of daily life: crafts, sciences, technology, trade, philosophy, food…
- English vocabulary was enriched by numerous **borrowings** from other languages. Between 1500 and 1650, over 10,000 new words entered the language (though many later fell out of use). Some 'purists' (who disliked change) opposed the introduction of new words.

Use a dictionary to find where the words for common foods came from: coffee, tea, tomato, chocolate, potato…

- Shakespeare therefore lived through a time when the English vocabulary was expanding amazingly and the grammar was still flexible, a time when people were intensely excited by language.

Shakespeare's plays reflect this fascination for words. Do some research to find examples of: Feste's wit in *Twelfth Night*; Dogberry's slip-ups in *Much Ado About Nothing*; Shylock's fatal bond and Portia's 'escape clause' in *The Merchant of Venice*; the puzzling oracle in *The Winter's Tale*, and Mistress Quickly's problems with words in *Henry V*.

Plays and playhouses

The theatre was a very popular form of entertainment in Shakespeare's time, with audiences drawn from all classes of people. The theatre buildings and the companies of actors were different from what we are used to today.

The theatres

- The professional theatre was based exclusively in London, which had around 200,000 inhabitants in 1600.
- It was always under attack from the **Puritan**-dominated Guildhall, which wanted to abolish the theatres totally because, in their opinion, they encouraged sinful behaviour.
- Acting companies first performed in the courtyards of coaching inns, in the halls of great houses, at markets and in the streets. The first outdoor playhouse as the Red Lion, built around 1567; and the first purpose-built theatre was The Theatre, Shoreditch, opened in 1576 (when Shakespeare was twelve).
- By 1600, there were eleven public outdoor theatres, including **the Rose**, the Swan and the Globe (Shakespeare's theatre).
- **Shakespeare's Globe** opened in 1599 on Maiden Lane, Bankside, and was destroyed by fire during a performance of *Henry VIII* in 1613. (No one was killed, but a bottle of ale was needed to put out a fire in a man's breeches!) See pages 166–168.
- Some outdoor theatres held audiences of up to 3,000.
- Standing room was one penny; the gallery two pence; the 'Lords' Room' three pence; and it was more expensive still to sit on the stage. This was at a time when a joiner (skilled carpenter) might earn 6 to 8 shillings (72 to 96 pence) per week. By 1614, it was six old pennies (2½ pence) for the newly opened indoor Hope Theatre.

Work out whether it was cheaper or more expensive to go to the theatre in Shakespeare's time than it is today. (To do the comparison, you will need to find out (a) how much the cheapest and most expensive tickets are at the Royal Shakespeare Theatre, Stratford-upon-Avon, for example; and (b) what a skilled worker might earn nowadays.)

- Outdoor theatre performances usually started at about 2 p.m. or 3 p.m. (there was no artificial light).
- The season started in September, through to the beginning of Lent; then from after Easter to early summer. (Theatres were closed in summer because of the increased risk of **plague**. Eleven thousand died of the plague in summer 1593 and the theatres remained almost completely closed until 1594.) Some companies went on summer tours, playing in inns, and similar places.
- All theatres were closed during the **Civil War** in 1642 (and most were demolished by 1656).
- There were some indoor theatres (called 'private' or 'hall' theatres) such as the **Blackfriars**, which was used up to 1609 almost exclusively by child actors (the entrance fee of sixpence indicates a wealthier audience). Plays developed which were more suited to the more intimate atmosphere, with the stage illuminated by artificial lighting.
- The star actor **Richard Burbage** and his brother Cuthbert had the licence of the Blackfriars from 1608 and Shakespeare's later plays were performed there.

Work out from the chart on pages 180–181 which of Shakespeare's plays might have been written with the indoor Blackfriars Theatre in mind.

The actors

- In 1572 parliament passed an Act 'For the Punishment of Vagabonds'. As actors were classed as little better than wandering beggars, this Act required them to be attached to a theatre company and have the **patronage** (financial support and protection) of someone powerful. This meant that companies had to keep on the right side of patrons and make sure they didn't offend the Master of the Revels, who was responsible for **censorship**.
- Major companies in Shakespeare's time included The Admiral's Men and The Queen's Men. **The Lord Chamberlain's Men** (the group that Shakespeare joined, later known as **The King's Men** when James came to the throne) was formed in 1594 and was run by shareholders (called 'the housekeepers').
- The Burbages held 50 per cent of the shares of the company; the remaining 50 per cent was divided mainly between the actors including Shakespeare himself, who owned between 10 and 12 per cent which helped to earn him a comfortable regular income.

Acting

- There was very little rehearsal time, with several plays 'in repertory' (being performed) in any given period.
- We don't actually know about the style of acting, but modern, naturalistic, low-key acting was probably not possible on the Globe stage. At the same time, Shakespeare appears to be mocking over-the-top delivery in at least two of his plays.

Read *Hamlet* 3.2 (Hamlet's first three speeches to the First Player).

- Actors certainly needed to be aware of their relationship with the audience: there must have been plenty of direct contact. In a daylight theatre there can be no pretence that the audience is not there.

Publishing

- Plays were not really regarded as 'literature' in Shakespeare's lifetime, and so the playwright would not have been interested in publishing his plays in book form.
- Some of Shakespeare's plays were, however, originally printed in cheap 'quarto' (pocket-size) editions. Some were sold officially (under an agreement made between the theatre company and the author), and some pirated (frequently by the actors themselves who had learned most of the script by heart).
- In 1623, seven years after Shakespeare's death, two of his close friends, John Heminge (or Heminges) and Henry Condell, collected together the most reliable versions of the plays and published them in a larger size volume known as the **First Folio**. This included eighteen plays which had never before appeared in print, and eighteen more which had appeared in quarto editions. Only *Pericles* was omitted from the plays which make up what we nowadays call Shakespeare's 'Complete Works' (unless we count plays such as *Two Noble Kinsmen*, which Shakespeare is known to have written in collaboration with another writer).

Much of the information in these sections comes from Michael Mangan, *A Preface to Shakespeare's Comedies: 1594–1603*, Longman, 1996.

The Globe Theatre

No one knows precisely what Shakespeare's Globe theatre looked like, but we do have a number of clues:

- a section of the foundations has been unearthed and provides a good idea of the size and shape of the outside walls
- the foundations of **the Rose**, a theatre near Shakespeare's, have been completely excavated
- a Dutch visitor to Shakespeare's London called Johannes de Witt saw a play in the Swan theatre and made a sketch of the interior (see below).

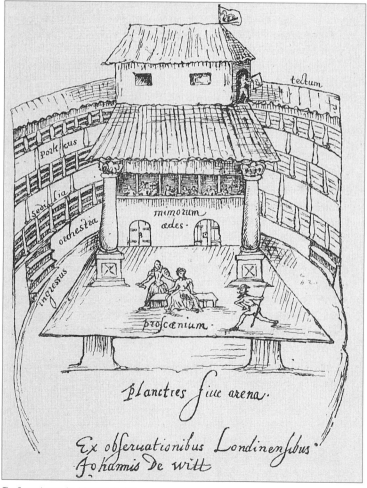

The Swan theatre, by Johannes de Witt

Using all the evidence available, a reconstruction of Shakespeare's Globe theatre has been built in London, not far from the site of the original building.

A *The facts*

From what you can learn from these photographs:

1. Roughly what shape is the theatre, looked at from above?
2. How many storeys does it have?
3. In which areas can the audience (a) stand and (b) sit?
4. What is behind the stage?
5. How much scenery and lighting are used?
6. What other details can you pick out which seem to make the Globe different from an indoor theatre (which has a stage at one end, similar to many school assembly halls)?

B *Using the stage*

Copy the plan on page 168. Then, using the staging guidelines provided, sketch or mark characters as they might appear at crucial moments in *A Midsummer Night's Dream* (such as Egeus's words with Theseus in 1.1).

C *The actor–audience relationship*

- In what ways is the design of Shakespeare's Globe ideally suited to the performance of his plays?
- How might the open stage and the balcony be useful? (Refer to moments in *A Midsummer Night's Dream* or other Shakespeare plays that you know.)
- What do you think would be the most interesting features of the way in which Shakespeare's actors – and those on the reconstructed Globe today – might relate to and interact with the audience? (Which moments in *A Midsummer Night's Dream* seem to require a performance in which the audience are very close to the actors, for example?)

Background to Shakespeare and *A Midsummer Night's Dream*

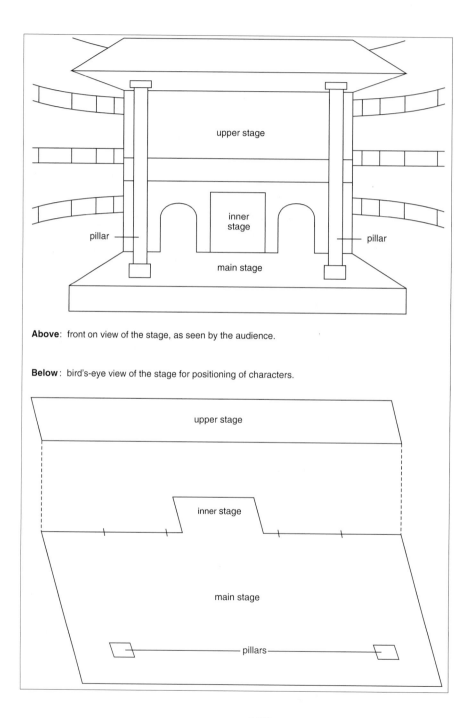

Above: front on view of the stage, as seen by the audience.

Below: bird's-eye view of the stage for positioning of characters.

The social background

Parents and children in Shakespeare's plays

- Many of Shakespeare's plays show conflicts between parents and their children, especially fathers and daughters. In many of the societies that Shakespeare describes, daughters seem to be regarded as property to be given in marriage to the most suitable young man who comes along.
- You can gain a good idea of the power that fathers had in Shakespeare's plays by looking up the following:
  - *Romeo and Juliet* in which Juliet's father violently threatens to throw her out on to the streets if she refuses to marry the man he has chosen (3.5)
  - *The Taming of the Shrew* in which Baptista refuses to allow his younger daughter to marry until someone has married his older daughter, Kate (1.1)
  - *King Lear* in which the old king casts off his youngest daughter, Cordelia, because she refuses to declare her love for him publicly (1.1)
  - *The Merchant of Venice*, in which Portia is not allowed by the terms of her dead father's will to make her own choice of a husband (1.2)
  - *Cymbeline*, in which the king refuses to let his daughter Innogen (sometimes called Imogen) marry the man she loves (1.2).

Fairies and magic

It was the Victorians in the nineteenth century who created the image of fairies as dainty girls with diaphanous wings; in Shakespeare's time they were regarded very differently and many people were terrified of them. Ten years or so before Shakespeare wrote *A Midsummer Night's Dream*, Reginald Scot published a book called *Discovery of Witchcraft*, in which he wrote:

'The Fairies do principally inhabit the mountains and caverns of the earth, whose nature is to make strange apparitions in the earth, in meadows or on mountains, being like men and women, soldiers kings and ladies, children and horsemen, clothed in green…

Such jocund and facetious spirits are said to sport themselves in the night by tumbling and fooling with servants and shepherds in country houses, pinching them black and blue…

And many such have been taken away by the said spirits for a fortnight or a month together…till at last they have been found lying in some meadow or mountain, bereaved of their senses, and commonly one of their members to boot…'

Classical mythology in the play

There are many references to ancient Greek and Roman mythology in *A Midsummer Night's Dream*. Shakespeare's audiences would have recognised the names and known the stories attached to them, but today we are less familiar with classical mythology. The following details will help you to understand the references and see what their relevance is when characters use them.

(Confusingly, the Romans gave new names to the gods when they took them over from the Greeks. Shakespeare tends to use the Roman name, but the Greek version has been added in brackets.)

The most important gods were the Olympians (so called because they lived on Mount Olympus). These included:
- Venus (Aphrodite), goddess of love (1.1.169)
- Neptune (Poseidon), god of the sea (2.1.126, 3.2.392)
- Apollo, god of young men, the arts and archery (2.1.230)
- Bacchus (Dionysus), god of wine – a later addition to Olympus (5.1.48).

The most important goddess referred to in the play is:
- Diana (Artemis), goddess of chastity, hunting and the moon (1.1.89, 2.1.163, 3.1.192, 4.1.73); by Shakespeare's time Diana was sometimes identified with the goddess Hecate (5.1.370).

The most important other immortal referred to is:
- Cupid (Eros), Venus's son, the archer-god (1.1.169, 2.1.159, 3.2.103).

Other immortals included:
- Phoebe and Phoebus, names for the moon and sun (1.1.209, 1.2.31)
- Aurora, the goddess of the dawn (3.2.380, 5.1.193)
- the Fates, three women who spun out each person's thread of life, including Atropos, who cut the thread (5.1.191 and 327)
- the Furies, who hounded wrong-doers (5.1.273).

There are also a number of mortals referred to, including:
- Theseus, who killed the Minotaur
- Hippolyta, Queen of the Amazons, a race of warrior women
- Æneas the Trojan who deserted his lover Dido, Queen of Carthage (1.1.173)
- Hercules (Heracles), one of the greatest of all heroes (1.2.25, 4.1.112, 5.1.44)
- Daphne, who was pursued by Apollo, but spirited away by the gods, who left a laurel tree in her place (2.1.230)
- Philomela, turned into a nightingale as she fled from her murderous husband (2.2.13)
- Cadmus, the founder of the city of Thebes (4.1.112)

- the beautiful Helen of Troy, who ran away from her husband with Prince Paris and precipitated the Trojan War (5.1.11)
- the Centaurs, creatures half-man and half-horse (5.1.44)
- Orpheus, the musician, torn apart by drunken women worshipping Bacchus (5.1.48)
- Leander, who swam the Hellespont to see his lover, Hero (5.1.191)
- Procris, accidentally killed by her husband Cephalus (she followed him hunting and he threw a spear at her, taking her for an animal: 5.1.193).

Places mentioned include Athens itself and Acheron, a river in Hades, the place of the dead (3.2.357).

Shakespeare's verse

Metre

It is possible to describe where the heavy stress falls in any English word. For example, these three words (from 1.1) have their heavy stress on the first syllable: **hap**py, **ling**ers, **quick**ly; while in these the heavy stress is on the second syllable: a**pace**, me**thinks**, de**sires**.

All Shakespeare's verse has a pattern of light and heavy stresses running through it, known as the metre. You can hear the metre if you read these lines aloud, over-emphasising the heavily stressed syllables:
- A**gainst** my **child**, my **dau**ghter, **Herm**ia (1.1.23)
- To **you** your **fa**ther **should** be **as** a **god** (1.1.47)
- To **live** a **bar**ren **sis**ter **all** your **life** (1.1.72).

No actor would ever perform the lines in that monotonous way, but they would certainly be aware that the metre was always there, helping to give the verse form and structure.

Sometimes, to point out that a syllable which does not carry a heavy stress in modern English is stressed in Shakespeare's line of verse, it will be accented, like this:
- Anon his Thisby must be answeréd (3.2.18).

1. Mark the heavy stresses in that line of Puck's (3.2.18).
2. Those four lines are all totally regular in their metre: what do you notice about (a) the pattern of short and heavy stresses? (b) the number of syllables?

171

Varying the metre

Most of the lines in Shakespeare's plays are not as regular as the three quoted above. In fact, most will have an irregular stress pattern, like this one, where two heavy stresses fall significantly together on the opening words 'Ill' and 'met':
- **Ill met** by **moon**light, **proud** Titania (2.1.60).

Occasionally a line will contain an extra syllable (11 rather than 10):
- When thou hast stolen away from fairy land (2.1.65).

Here the actor can either try to deliver 'stolen' as one syllable (stol'n), or emphasise the word by retaining both syllables.

Some lines really stand out, because they are clearly short:
- It is my lord. (4.1.137).

Here Egeus's reply is brief and to the point.

A collection of heavy stresses together can add emphasis:
- **From our** de**bate**, **from our** dis**sen**sion (2.1.116)

Dividing the line into feet

Just as music has a number of beats in a bar, so Shakespeare's verse has five 'feet' in a complete line. A five-feet line is called 'pentameter' (pent = five; metre = measure).

A single foot can contain syllables from different words, and any one word can be broken up by the foot divisions:
- In mai | -den med | -ita | -tion fan | -cy free (2.1.164).

This is why a single line of verse is sometimes set out rather oddly in different lines of print, if it is shared between two or more characters, as happens in 3.2:

PUCK	Here villain, drawn and ready. Where art thou?	line 402
LYSANDER	I will be with thee straight	} line
PUCK	Follow me, then,	} 403
	To plainer ground.	} line
DEMETRIUS	Lysander, speak again;	} 404

Iambic pentameter

A foot which contains an unstressed syllable followed by a stressed one (the standard 'beat': dee-**dum**) is called an 'iamb'. Verse which has five iambs per line as its standard rhythm is called 'iambic pentameter'.

Iambic pentameter which does not rhyme is also sometimes known as 'blank verse'.

1. Bearing in mind that the iambic pentameter line goes: dee-**dum**, dee-**dum**, dee-**dum**, dee-**dum**, dee-**dum**, make up some of your own 'Shakespearean' verse (perhaps based on one of the themes of the play, such as love).
2. Copy out the following lines from 1.1 and divide them into five feet; then mark the heavy stresses: 30, 42, 52, 72 and (more difficult) 83.
3. Do the same with these key lines: 1.1.134, 1.1.234, 2.1.242, 2.1.249, 3.2.388. Pick one and show how the rhythm helps the meaning.

Rhyme

A Midsummer Night's Dream contains a great deal of rhyming verse. Most of it is rhyming iambic pentameter:

I know a bank whereon the wild thyme blows;
Where oxlips and the nodding violet grows (2.1.249–250).

But Puck's and Oberon's speeches are often in rhyming lines of four stresses (see page 40):

Night and silence: who is here?
Weeds of Athens he doth wear: (2.2.69–70).

The fairy in 2.1 moves from two-stress lines (2.1.2–5), through four-stresses (6–15) to pentameter (16–17), all in rhyme.

Shakespeare sometimes uses rhyme for the ends of scenes or sections of scenes, where a 'rhyming couplet' can have the effect of rounding things off. This happens in 2.1, where Helena concludes her impassioned pleading with two couplets:

We cannot fight for love, as men may do;
We should be wooed, and were not made to woo.
I'll follow thee, and make a heaven of hell,
To die upon the hand I love so well. (2.1.241–244).

Find other scenes or sections of scenes which end with a rhyming couplet and discuss what the effect might be in each case.

Verse and prose

It is never totally clear why Shakespeare chooses to write some scenes, or passages, in verse, and others in prose.

Although there are many examples where the more serious scenes, involving great passions, are in verse while those about ordinary people and comedy are in prose, there are also significant examples throughout Shakespeare's plays where this is not the case.

Look back through *A Midsummer Night's Dream* and try to work out why certain scenes are in verse and others in prose.

The plot of *A Midsummer Night's Dream*

Act 1

1.1: As Theseus and Hippolyta are discussing their coming wedding day, Egeus enters with his daughter, Hermia, and two young men, Lysander and Demetrius. Egeus is angry that Hermia is rejecting his choice of a husband, Demetrius, in favour of Lysander, and he invokes an ancient law, which Theseus supports: Hermia must marry Demetrius, become a nun or be executed. Left alone, Lysander and Hermia bemoan their thwarted love, but Lysander has an idea: they can run away and stay with his aunt, who lives seven leagues from Athens, and there they can get married. When Helena enters, miserable because her love for Demetrius is not being returned, they comfort her by explaining their plan. Left to herself, Helena decides that she will reveal the plan to Demetrius, to win his favour.

1.2: A group of workmen ('mechanicals') meet to rehearse a play, which they hope to perform as part of the Duke's wedding celebrations. Peter Quince informs them that the play is 'Pyramus and Thisby', a tragic love story, and he allocates parts. Nick Bottom is pleased to be given the role of the hero, Pyramus, but, when he hears that Francis Flute is to play Thisby in a mask, he wants to take on that role too. Robin Starveling and Tom Snout are given their parts and Bottom once again tries to persuade Quince – without success – to let him play someone else's part, this time Snug the joiner's role of the lion. Quince persuades Bottom to stick with Pyramus and they all agree to meet the next night in the wood outside the palace, where they can rehearse without being bothered by on-lookers.

Act 2

2.1: In the wood, Puck accosts a fairy serving the fairy Queen Titania. Puck warns the fairy to keep out of the way, as Titania and the King of the fairies, Oberon, are in dispute: Oberon is demanding a little Indian boy that Titania has adopted, and she is refusing to give him up. The fairy recognises Puck, who admits to some of his pranks, and then Titania and Oberon enter. They have come to give joy and prosperity to the marriage between Theseus and Hippolyta, but their own dispute has resulted in the seasons being turned upside-down, and wet, wintery weather blighting the countryside. Titania storms off, refusing once more to give up the boy, and Oberon plots with Puck to gain his revenge and get what he wants. He asks Puck to fetch a flower called love-in-idleness. It contains a magic juice which, if placed on a sleeper's eyelids, will cause them to fall in love with the first thing they see on awaking. Oberon plans to use it on Titania, in the hope that she will fall in love with something repulsive and, in her infatuated state, give up the boy to him.

In the middle of his plotting, Demetrius enters, followed by Helena. He is seeking Hermia and angrily spurns Helena as he rushes off to continue his search. Watching the scene, Oberon takes pity on Helena and plans to turn the tables on Demetrius. When Puck returns, he tells him to find the disdainful Athenian youth and anoint his eyes. Meanwhile, Oberon will do the same to Titania.

2.2: After Titania has ordered her fairies to sing her asleep, Oberon enters and anoints her eyes with the love-juice. He leaves her sleeping and Lysander and Hermia enter. Lysander has lost their way and they agree to sleep here for the night. They settle down and Puck enters. He spies Lysander and, thinking that this is the youth referred to by Oberon, he anoints his eyes. When Helena enters and, in her surprise at seeing him, wakes Lysander, he immediately falls in love with her. Assuming that he is mocking her with false declarations of his love, she runs off and Lysander follows, leaving Hermia asleep. When Hermia awakes after a nightmare and finds Lysander gone, she desperately runs off to try to find him.

Act 3

3.1: The mechanicals enter the same part of the wood, to rehearse their play. Bottom is concerned that the ladies in the palace audience will be shocked to see Pyramus kill himself, and Quince agrees to his suggestion that a prologue should be written which explains that the killing is not for real and that Pyramus is actually Bottom the weaver. There is also a concern that the ladies will be frightened of the lion, and they agree to another idea from Bottom that Snug should reassure the audience and explain who he is.

Quince himself then raises two difficulties. The first is how to bring moonlight into the chamber and it is decided that someone must represent the figure of moonshine. The second problem concerns what to do about the wall which divides the lovers in the play. Bottom again saves the day with the idea that someone can actually play the part of Wall.

With these problems resolved, they begin their rehearsal. But Puck has entered and decides to cause mischief. When Bottom goes off-stage, Puck fixes an ass's head upon him. Bottom returns, unaware of his transformation, and the mechanicals run off in terror. Bottom thinks they are trying to trick him into being scared and, to keep his spirits up, he starts to sing. Titania awakes and immediately falls in love with him. She calls her attendant fairies in and they lead Bottom to her bower.

3.2: Puck delightedly tells Oberon what has happened to Titania and how the mechanicals were terrorised. But when Hermia enters pursued by Demetrius, Puck admits that this is not the man he anointed. Hermia runs off and the exhausted Demetrius sleeps, giving Oberon the opportunity to anoint his eyes with the love-juice, while Puck goes off to fetch Helena. She soon enters, followed by the love-sick Lysander and the sound of their voices causes Demetrius to awake. As planned, he falls in love with Helena, who is now wooed by both men. She assumes that they are mocking her and, when Hermia enters, only to be rejected by Lysander, Helena begins to believe that her friend is part of the plot against her too and she reminds Hermia of their childhood friendship.

But Hermia is also baffled: she cannot understand why Lysander is spurning her in favour of Helena, nor why Helena is accusing her of plotting against her with the men. When Lysander insults Hermia, she finally accepts that his rejection of her is for real and she turns on Helena, accusing her of stealing Lysander's love. When Lysander and Demetrius march off to fight, Helena runs away, afraid of what Hermia might do to her, and then Hermia leaves the scene too. Oberon rebukes Puck for causing such confusion and orders him to prevent the men from fighting and then to anoint Lysander's eyes with the antidote to the love-juice. As Lysander and Demetrius try to pursue each other, Puck imitates each one's voice and ensures that they do not meet up by luring them to different parts of the wood. One by one the four lovers enter, exhausted, and fall asleep on the ground. Puck anoints Lysander's eyes with the antidote and leaves them sleeping.

Act 4

4.1: As Oberon watches unseen, Bottom enters, being pampered by Titania. They fall asleep and Oberon explains to Puck how he met Titania in the woods and mocked her. She has given up the boy and now Oberon is prepared to restore her to normality. He anoints her eyes with the antidote and, when she awakes to recall her 'dream', he explains to her what has happened. As they dance, now happily reunited after their arguments, Puck removes the ass's head and they all depart.

Theseus and Hippolyta have entered the wood for a morning's hunting and discover the four sleeping lovers. Theseus orders them to be awoken and Lysander is forced to explain that he and Hermia had planned to run away and get married. Egeus is furious, but Demetrius reveals that he now loves Helena again and Theseus overrides Egeus's wishes: the two couples will be married when he weds Hippolyta.

As everyone returns to Athens, the lovers still bewildered by their experiences, Bottom wakes up. He tries to recall the amazing dream he has just had and determines to get Peter Quince to turn it into a ballad.

4.2: The rest of the mechanicals are despondent: Bottom is still missing and, without him, the play cannot go on. But Bottom arrives to urge them to get ready as their play has been short-listed for the wedding celebrations.

Act 5

5.1: Theseus finds the lovers' accounts of their night's experiences difficult to believe, but Hippolyta is impressed by the consistency of their accounts. Philostrate presents Theseus with a list of all the entertainments on offer and tries to put him off when he chooses the mechanicals' play. When Theseus insists, Hippolyta expresses her reservations. She does not want to see the men make fools of themselves, but Theseus is prepared to accept their offering as an act of duty. Quince begins the play with a halting prologue and then describes what happens in the story, pointing out the characters as he does so. After Snout has entered to announce himself as Wall, Bottom comes in as Pyramus and curses the wall when he fails to see his love, Thisby. But she then enters, played by Flute, and the lovers speak through the chink, agreeing to meet at 'Ninny's' (Ninus's) tomb.

Wall exits and the lion enters to explain that he is actually Snug the joiner. He is joined by Starveling, who carries the lantern, dog and bush of thorns which signify that he is the man in the moon. Starveling becomes flustered when the court audience interrupt him, but Thisby enters on cue to be chased off by the lion, dropping her mantle as she flees. Pyramus enters, finds the mantle, stained with blood from the lion's mouth, and, believing Thisby to be dead, stabs himself.

Thisby enters to find her dead lover and kills herself with his sword. As the audience comment on the ending, Bottom leaps up to offer them either an epilogue or a dance. Theseus hastily opts for the dance, the mechanicals perform it, and the stage clears.

Puck enters with a broom to sweep the dust behind the door, and then Oberon and Titania bless the marriages of the three couples. Puck concludes the play with a request for applause.

Study skills: titles and quotations

Referring to titles

When you are writing an essay, you will often need to refer to the title of the play. There are two main ways of doing this:

- If you are hand-writing your essay, the title of the play should be underlined: <u>A Midsummer Night's Dream</u>
- If you are word-processing your essay, the play title should be in italics: *A Midsummer Night's Dream*.

The same rules apply to titles of all plays and other long works including novels and non-fiction, such as: *Animal Farm* and *The Diary of Anne Frank*. The titles of poems or short stories are placed inside single inverted commas; for example: 'Timothy Winters' and 'A Sound of Thunder'.

Note that the first word in a title and all the main words will have capital (or 'upper case') letters, while the less important words (such as conjunctions, prepositions and articles) will usually begin with lower case letters; for example: *The Taming of the Shrew* or *Antony and Cleopatra*.

Using quotations

Quotations show that you know the play in detail and are able to produce evidence from the script to back up your ideas and opinions. It is usually a good idea to keep quotations as short as you can (and this especially applies to exams, where it is a waste of time copying chunks out of the script).

Using longer quotations

There are a number of things you should do if you want to use a quotation of more than a few words:

1. Make your point. ——— Lysander seems to be willing to stand up for himself: *2. A colon introduces the quotation.*

3. Leave a line.

4. Indent the quotation. ——— I am, my Lord, as well derived as he,   *5. No quotation marks.*
As well possessed; my love is more than his...

6. Keep the same line-divisions as the script.   *7. Three dots show that the quotation is incomplete*

8. Continue with a ——— Lysander stresses his birth...
follow-up point, perhaps commenting on the quotation itself.

Using brief quotations

Brief quotations are usually easier to use, take less time to write out and are much more effective in showing how familiar you are with the play. Weave them into the sentence like this:

- Pointing out that Demetrius had 'Made love to Nedar's daughter, Helena', Lysander argues that...

If you are asked to state where the quotation comes from, use this simple form of reference to indicate the Act, scene and line:

- When Titania calls Oberon's claims 'the forgeries of jealousy' (2.1.81), she is...

In some editions this is written partly in Roman numerals – upper case for the Act and lower case for the scene; for example: (II.i.81), or (II.1.81).

William Shakespeare and *A Midsummer Night's Dream*

No one knows for sure when *A Midsummer Night's Dream* was written, but it was referred to in a book published in 1598, and so must have been written before that date. The theatres were closed because of plague during most of 1593 and 1594, and most people believe that the play was written just before or just after that period.

Shakespeare's life and career

No one is absolutely sure when Shakespeare wrote each play.

1564 Born in Stratford-upon-Avon, first son of John and Mary Shakespeare.
1582 Marries Anne Hathaway from the nearby village of Shottery. She is 8 years older and expecting their first child.
1583 Daughter Susannah born.
1585 Twin son and daughter, Hamnet and Judith, born.

Some time before **1592** Shakespeare arrives in London, becomes an actor and writes poems and plays. Several plays are performed, probably including the three parts of *Henry VI*. Another writer, Robert Greene, writes about 'Shake-scene', the 'upstart crow' who has clearly become a popular playwright.

By **1595** he is a shareholder with the Lord Chamberlain's Men (see page 164) and has probably written *Richard III, Comedy of Errors, Titus Andronicus, The Taming of the Shrew, The Two Gentlemen of Verona, Love's Labours Lost, Romeo and Juliet, Richard II* and *A Midsummer Night's Dream* (as well as contributing to plays by other writers and writing the poems 'Venus and Adonis' and 'The Rape of Lucrece').

1596 Hamnet dies, age 11.
1597 Buys New Place, one of the finest houses in Stratford.
1599 Globe Theatre opens on Bankside.

By **1599**: *King John, The Merchant of Venice*, the two parts of *Henry IV, The Merry Wives of Windsor, Much Ado About Nothing, Julius Caesar* and *Henry V* (as well as the Sonnets).

1603 King James I grants the Lord Chamberlain's Men a Royal Patent and they become The King's Men (page 164).

By **1608**: *As You Like It, Hamlet, Twelfth Night, Troilus and Cressida, All's Well That Ends Well, Measure For Measure, Othello, Macbeth, King Lear, Antony and Cleopatra, Pericles, Coriolanus* and *Timon of Athens*.

1608 The King's Men begin performing plays in the indoor Blackfriars Theatre (page 164).

By **1613**: *Cymbeline, The Winter's Tale, The Tempest, Henry VIII, Two Noble Kinsmen* (the last two probably with John Fletcher).

1616 Dies, April 23, and is buried in Holy Trinity Church, Stratford.
1623 Publication of the First Folio (page 165).

Shakespeare's times

1558 Elizabeth I becomes queen.

1565 The explorer John Hawkins introduces sweet potatoes and tobacco into England.

1567 Mary Queen of Scots abdicates in favour of her year-old son, James VI.

1568 Mary escapes to England and is imprisoned by Elizabeth.

1572 Francis Drake attacks Spanish ports in the Americas.

1576 James Burbage opens the first theatre (The Theatre) in London.

1580 Francis Drake returns from a circumnavigation of the world.

1582 Pope Gregory reforms the Christian calendar.

1587 Mary Queen of Scots executed for a treasonous plot against Elizabeth; Drake partly destroys the Spanish fleet at Cádiz and war breaks out with Spain.

1588 Philip II of Spain's Armada is destroyed by the English fleet.

1592 Plague kills 20,000 Londoners.

1593 Playwright Christopher Marlowe killed in a pub brawl.

1596 Tomatoes introduced into England; John Harington invents the water-closet (the ancestor of the modern lavatory).

1597 Earl of Tyrone leads a new rebellion in Ireland.

1599 Earl of Essex concludes a truce with Tyrone, returns home and is arrested.

1601 Essex is tried and executed for treasonous plots against Elizabeth.

1603 Elizabeth I dies and is succeeded by James VI of Scotland as James I of England.
Sir Walter Raleigh is jailed for plotting against James.

1604 James is proclaimed 'King of Great Britain, France and Ireland'; new church rules cause 300 Puritan clergy to resign.

1605 Gunpowder Plot uncovered.

1607 First permanent European settlement in America at Jamestown, Virginia.

1610 Galileo looks at the stars through a telescope; tea is introduced into Europe.

1611 Authorised Version of the Bible.

1618 Raleigh executed for treason.
Physician William Harvey announces discovery of blood circulation.

1620 Pilgrim Fathers sail from Plymouth to colonise America.

1625 James I dies and is succeeded by Charles I.

Index to activities

Character reviews

Bottom	20, 54, 64, 98, 99, 116, 138, 155–156
Character profiles	154–155
Egeus	110
Helena	12, 24, 48, 80
Hermia	4, 50
Hermia, Helena, Lysander and Demetrius	157–158
Hippolyta	118
Oberon	40, 72, 104
Oberon, Titania and the fairies	156–157
Peter Quince	22, 150
Philostrate	124
Puck	26, 28, 74, 98, 156
Quince, Flute, Snout, Starveling, Snug, Theseus, Hippolyta, Egeus, Philostrate	158
The lovers	76, 78, 112
The mechanicals	18, 24–25, 118
Theseus	6, 110
Theseus and Hippolyta	120, 124
Titania	106

Plot reviews

News from court	8–10
The lovers	25, 76, 96, 98
Who loves whom?	46
Events in the wood	52
A strand chart	53
Puck's mischief	68
Puck's assignments	90
Surveying 3.2	94
Hermia's choice	108
Acrostic	160
Mini-saga	160
Sonnet	160

Themes

Dreams · 92, 160

Love · 2, 4, 14, 25, 44, 52, 53, 64, 99, 108, 118, 119, 159

Order and disorder · 32–34, 70, 146, 150–151, 160

Theatrical illusion · 58–60, 120, 134, 148, 159

Shakespeare's language

A poster · 159

Language effects · 159

Language variety · 159

Magic spells · 42

Malapropisms · 56

Mixed senses · 112

Mythology · 25

Names · 16

'Now the lion hungry roars…' · 144

Oberon's changing mood · 106

One-line speeches · 12

Shakespearian insults · 88

'Sweet moon…' · 138

The mechanicals · 24

The moon · 2

The unused epilogue · 142

'…the prologue is addressed' · 126

Actors' interpretations · 8, 22, 30, 36, 38, 42, 44, 50, 62, 66, 70, 72, 78, 82, 84, 86, 90, 94, 96, 100, 102, 114, 122, 128, 130, 132, 136, 140, 144, 150, 152–154